Kim,

This Book was written from the inside out. From within me came the songs, then the poems, then the website, then the book.

The Book itself looks back at the music and poems, and offers context, perspective and "Inspiration"

So "Inspiration" is where it all started, and where the book ends; at what I hope is yet another inspiration for my readers and listeners...

...From the Inside Out!

Peace! Chris

AS I SEE IT

Reasons, Rhymes, and Reflections;
The Spirit of a "Well-Versed" Philosophy

CHRIS MENTCH

WESTBOW
PRESS®
A DIVISION OF THOMAS NELSON
& ZONDERVAN

WestBow Press books may be ordered through booksellers or by contacting:

WestBow Press
A Division of Thomas Nelson & Zondervan
1663 Liberty Drive
Bloomington, IN 47403
www.westbowpress.com
1 (866) 928-1240

Because of the dynamic nature of the Internet, any web addresses or links contained in this book may have changed since publication and may no longer be valid. The views expressed in this work are solely those of the author and do not necessarily reflect the views of the publisher, and the publisher hereby disclaims any responsibility for them.

Any people depicted in stock imagery provided by Thinkstock are models, and such images are being used for illustrative purposes only. Certain stock imagery © Thinkstock.

ISBN: 978-1-5127-0997-1 (sc)
ISBN: 978-1-5127-0998-8 (hc)
ISBN: 978-1-5127-0996-4 (e)

Library of Congress Control Number: 2015913814

Print information available on the last page.

WestBow Press rev. date: 9/2/2015

CONTENTS

DEDICATION

Dedicated to Chisum

For his grace, his glory and his limitless and other-worldly ability to
carry The Spirit upon his broad, loving and able wings – Forever soar
in peace dear brother. I am eternally yours.

Epigraph

"I believe that ideology is like a roadmap; it can act as a guide, but if held too close, it can obscure reality and the true path that lies ahead."
– Chris Mentch

FOREWORD

Foreword by Daniel M. Cislo, Esq.

As I See It is a beautiful look into the multi-faceted mind of its author to lift the spirits of all who read it. So often we are consumed by factoids, blogs, posts and news, but *As I See It* is a refreshing deep-dive into the most important thoughts of life. It is a mixture of philosophy and pleasing verse to provide the salvation so needed in our stress-filled world.

Chris Mentch helps his readers reflect on what is truly valuable, and he reveals in himself a path of self-discovery which we can all follow. Rather than tell the reader what to think or how to view the world, Chris offers "reasons, rhymes, and reflections" to guide each of us on a journey of spiritual exploration and refocus of what is important, and I have no doubt that readers will take away many different experiences from *As I See It.*

To know Chris is to love his spirit, and his new book, *As I See It: Reasons, Rhymes, and Reflections; The Spirit of a "Well-Versed" Philosophy,* completely captures his essence so as to also lift your own spirits.

PREFACE

As an accomplished professional in the business world and CPA as well as an accomplished singer/songwriter of stage and studio I have a unique and broad range of experience that has given me a very valuable perspective and insight into the concerns of a diverse clientele and audience and the skill set to share it with you all here. *As I See It* is certainly not a policy or process book. It is a book written in a conversational tone, fit more for a sun-drenched beach or crackling fireside and is intended to give you, my readers, an intimate look and understanding of what I have learned in my broad professional experience in both business and music, communication and entertainment. I want this book to be as memorable and as much fun as your favorite song and as valuable as the best advice or perhaps insight you have ever gotten from a dear friend. It is written to quench some of the thirst of the human condition in a practical manner and is intended to be easily applicable to the everyday lives and aspirations of my readers.

I have excelled both academically as a *summa cum laude* graduate with multiple academic honors and honors of executive institutes and worked as a financial professional in the largest, most prestigious accounting and consulting firm in the world. My study and experience in these arenas provide me with solid grounding, establishing and maintaining a successful enterprise, setting and achieving goals and measuring success. The magical spark of this book however, is the blend of these attributes with the time I have spent face to face with members of my audiences; strangers to me at first, but quickly they became as familiar as neighbors. I am a student of the human condition as well as professional of two disciplines that when combined can offer practical observations and suggestions on what I have learned and how to apply them in the day to day. More importantly, it is through this exercise that I can offer to you the messages of what I've learned though the vehicle of my lyrics, as well as the experience and background of exactly where those lyrics came from, what they are intended to convey and why it is important to me, and of course to you.

My approach stems from my belief that we are all more the same than we are different, and this commonality is the bond of our society in that we are all in this together with much to share. However, I also maintain that it is our individual strengths that create a multi-faceted society and a diversely talented culture. In this free market democratic republic ideal of "America," these traits combined with our philosophical underpinning of a Judeo-Christian belief system, creates an exceptional nation that is the best hope for this beautiful planet, our lovely home, indeed our combined place, in the sky!

I am grateful for your kind time and it is my deep hope that after you read *As I See It* that you will feel much more like a friend of mine and much less like a reader. So, my new friend, let's get after it!

ACKNOWLEDGEMENT

Thank you to my family for allowing me to sing myself to sleep as a boy without once complaining and thanks to the stars above for remaining.

Thank you to all my teachers and professors for allowing me to grow intellectually by way of their caring and skill and talent.

Thank you to my fellow live stage band members and studio musicians with whom I shared the unique experience of giving the joy of music to listening audiences and thank you to the audiences for making it all magic.

Thank you to the love of my life for this eternal journey and the love we share for The Spirit that guides us.

Thank you to all my friends for your acceptance, your sharing, your input and the time we hold dear.

Special thanks to Diego Berber, "The Wizard of the Website" and my never-reluctant co-pilot.

Special thanks to Caleigh Garcia for her encouragement, guidance and experience and for casting me in her kindest light; for she is the conductor of a vast orchestra, who, with uncanny calm asks the sky, the wind and the sun's simmering fickle way, to sustain the moment… when my eyes open a path and give my soul to all of you.

Special thanks to Christopher Takahashi whose instinctual acumen for reflecting the soul and the passion through the style "takes it to the wall."

I am also very proud to acknowledge that headshot photography is the artwork courtesy of Joanna DeGeneres. All the world is a canvas for her instincts and skill. A master at capturing and presenting all that makes up the true core of a person, to anyone who, even for an instant, glances at her work. Thank you Jo.

Special Thanks also to Daniel M. Cislo, Esq. author of the forward of this book, for his passion, appreciation and dedication of his unmatched skill in protecting the labors of love that we create and his keen understanding of why we create them.

INTRODUCTION

Let me say thank you right at the start for reading *As I See It* which is, at its core, a vehicle for my writing that reflects my overall philosophy. The material is in the form of music, poetry and prose, journalized style as well as some backstory essays as well. It is my expression of my approach and outlook in dealing with a far ranging variety of the topics of our time. Within *As I See It* I cover issues from the matters of the heart and the concerns and passions we all share as individuals, to broader issues of our time such as issues of the environment, inter-personal dealings and societal implications, leadership roles, personal growth and inspiration just to name a few. It is a very broad range perhaps that could best be described as a love songbook meets *The Wall Street Journal* and a practical guide to problem solving and philosophy. So come hungry, there's a lot to chew on!

My attempt here is to share with you my approach to many varied issues in a way that addresses the specific day to day practical attributes of each topic, while at the same time addressing the over-arching philosophical context with which I see our roles in it all. I hope that you find it interesting, practical and refreshing and perhaps even a bit challenging.

Since life is enriched in sharing our experiences and stories, our thoughts and our memories, our aspirations and our dreams, it is my hope that as you explore and consider my work, it may open your eyes to something new or perhaps revive a distant memory. Maybe it will have you consider a different point of view, or maybe find that you are not as alone in your views as perhaps you thought you were on some topic. It is also my intention to create a space in each piece where a topic can be considered more deeply than our hectic lives often allow. For, if we are to live life deliberately, then we must allow time for true consideration, whether it be a particular event, or the experiences of a lifetime, a long held belief, or a new found approach. Since I am a firm believer that there is often a deeper meaning in what may seem commonplace occurrences, I'll touch on that here as well. Or, perhaps *As I See It* is simply where you might find a way to express how you may have felt at some time in your life when the right words just would not come.

In any and in all cases, I would ask you to simply consider this: That life is a beautiful, dramatic and deeply meaningful play, its ending as yet unwritten. Indeed, we are all characters in this story, but we are also its authors. We are, each of us, free to write the future upon the empty pages before us. They open at the dawn of every day; a newborn, full of possibilities and treasures. Our future awaits those of us who are willing to hold close the notion that we are all in this together. Our fates and our combined wisdom are intimately connected and it will serve us all well to remember that while we are each of us unique, we are all more the same than we are different. So, please be kind to one another.

I hope you will find something in the pages that follow to call your very own.

It is my pleasure to share these thoughts with you, *As I See It*.

Peace.

PROLOGUE

If You Look No Further...

My message is a simple one:

Seek your dreams.
Be responsible for being kind.
Challenge yourself to be the Hero you'd most admire.
The spirit is waiting within you.
Seek it.
      Embrace it.
           Nurture it.
                Share it.
Welcome to As I See It,

Seek it   *Embrace it*

Nurture it   *Share it.*

MUSIC IS

Music is a seeker and a giver. She seeks us out and finds us when we are most welcome to her, in whatever form we require. She answers the yearning within each of us to share, express our feelings and to be understood. She is a giver, when she quenches the thirst we all feel to understand each other and our relationship to one another and the garden we all share.

It is with music that we can explore the mysteries of life. We can find answers, as well as questions. And if we listen closely, we can find each other. — Chris

Songs Table of Contents

NAMASTE, THIS CHRISTMAS DAY

The term *Namaste*, refers to the act of the Spirit within one person acknowledging the Spirit in another. "The Spirit in me salutes the Spirit in you" since it is believed that we are all one in the eyes of a single divine consciousness. A place where the entire universe resides; a place where light, love, truth and peace are so common and fundamental to each of us, that we are indeed one when we, if not only our mindset, are there; a practice of the Hindus of the Indian subcontinent observing One Divine Consciousness at the center of it all. I find this personally to be a very healthy way of thinking, and yes, even in what we often call a dog-eat-dog world. In fact, *especially* in such a world. For it's exactly that kind of world that we often create. It follows, therefore, that if we created it, we are best suited to dismantle and reject it. This is not to suggest that there are not naturally competing forces at play in our lives, of course there are. However, to the extent we create and compound additional friction and division that is corrosive to our civil society and our future, we are certainly capable of refining our understanding and correcting the errors of our ways as we all move forward, together. I also believe that history is written in steps forward and steps backward. Again, a natural process for we learn as we go. We will not always make the proper choices every time but it's best we get better at it with each passing day. We are all equally capable of dark deeds and lovely ones; choose wisely.

I had never considered myself qualified to write a Christmas song as so many lovely ones have come before. It is such a time so rich in meaning and glory, my words couldn't do it justice. Then, once again, I stepped out of the way of the song, and the song came to me just as it was meant to be. I got the sense that it was patiently waiting for me to wise up, and see myself as part of the song, and took my humble place with, and among you all.

NAMASTE, THIS CHRISTMAS DAY

I seek the deepest brightest part of you
With one simple word all this I say.
To cast aside the struggles we've been through
for this I pray, for this I pray...

Namaste! Namaste!
I pray to The Spirit within you
That on this day, this Christmas Day
He finds us scattered strangers, and He binds us dear as friends.

I hear the distant bells are ringing
My nose just knows the snows will fall.
And I can hear the angels singing
With my childhood voice, just down the hall.

I'm bathed in Gloried Light and Splendor
My ears still test the silent skies.
For reindeer, sleighs and sweet surrender,
The joy and peace I still remember,
On candied air I taste surprise!

Namaste! Namaste!
I pray to The Spirit within you.
That on this day, this Christmas Day
He finds us scattered strangers, and He binds us dear as friends.

Just as the snowflakes we are many
And yet no two of us the same.
Each brings from heaven our sacred plenty,
To a single vision, of many names.

So let me take my place beside you
A space that only we can fill.
As we reflect the light and wonder,
And perfect the Grace we've fallen under,
On this Holy Night so still.

And, *Namaste! Namaste!*
I pray to The Spirit within you.
That on this day, this Christmas Day,
He finds us scattered strangers, and He binds us dear as friends.

The cold reminds me that I need you;
That time and tides roll on so fast.
Let's hold forever in this moment.
Let not what's in our reach, escape our grasp.

And, *Namaste! Namaste!*
I pray to The Spirit within you.
That on this day, this Christmas Day,
He finds us scattered strangers, and He binds us here....
He binds us as dear friends. . . . . "Do you hear what I hear?"

THE AMBER CRADLE OF FOREVER'S DAY – CHISUM'S SONG

We all learn when we ask meaningful questions. We all learn more deeply when our hunger for what we seek to know is more pronounced. Our awareness is heightened and our senses are aroused and exponentially more acute. We also know that it is axiomatic that nature abhors a vacuum. Therefore, given these attributes of filling some void, we can see that nature is the ultimate teacher and a consummate communicator. It is with this fundamental backdrop that I approach explaining to you just how the time I spent with a wild red tail hawk brought me the song "The Amber Cradle of Forever's Day."

I suppose that writing is akin to active recreation for me as well as my need to try to share the more meaningful aspects of living with anyone who is gracious enough with their time to listen. Expressing myself, in whatever way, completes my sense of what I am about and what I feel I can contribute in some small way. It completes my day like a sunset, and is as natural to me as breathing. Being outdoors and around nature's openness is the perfect stage for me to open up to what presents itself to me; I relax into it, and then write.

I had been trying to write a song that dealt with the passing of time, living and dying, hellos and goodbyes; all the linear and chronological events that come and go as we live our lives. There was however, a dissonance I felt in the "chronological and linear" aspects of what I was trying to communicate. The dissonance was the feeling that miracles happen in mere minutes and seconds and yet are preserved in memories, in learning from experience and in passing on what we know, what we love and celebrate, and how and what we choose to share. That seemed to fly in the face of the "tick-tock of mere events" that come and then go; start and expire. The song would come somewhat closer to me in a dream. At other times while I was awake. The dissonance of the message remained while the song came sometimes subtly, while at other times would rush me like a storm across a desert, yet always elusive, until. Yes! *A storm across a desert!* The *void* is the space between the storm and the desert. The *need* or the *yearning* was the thirst for water on the parched earth below. I looked up and there was *Chisum*, a wild red tail hawk that befriended me years ago. The *messenger* was that which walked upon the wind above me *the instant* the message became so clear. My singular focus on the detail of the song was untangled by Chisum's silent flight above. Wings outstretched as he held his place in the sky, easily low enough that I could see his eyes looking directly down at me. It was his presence that relaxed my senses to a place, perhaps like tuning me into the signal that I was capable of grasping if I could reach it. But the only way to reach it was to relax into it, have faith and trust it.

I had at that time been spending time with Chisum on hillsides in southern California for years. When we first met it was by surprise to me that he would fly near me and land closer and closer to me if I was in one place for any period of time. After I began speaking to him when he sat very close I named him Chisum, a name I borrowed from the John Wayne western of the same name. In the movie, Mr. Wayne's character was strong, insightful, measured yet capable of striking if need be in an instant. He was stoic and resolved, seasoned and wise, caring and courageous; the perfect name for my wind-walking brother.

Chisum's presence is to me best described as silent ground trembling thunder. Before you see him, you feel his distinct and unmistakable presence. The power of his spirit and his gift to me is the deepest spiritual feeling I have ever had before or since. It is undeniable. It is unstoppable. It is a force of true beautiful nature in its most vibrantly communicative way. There exists a purity of the message and the messenger.

"The Amber Cradle of Forever's Day" is about my opening up or awakening to a personal message from a divine Spirit. There is simply no other way to put it and no real reason to try. This song came to me in a manner not at all like any "process" of writing or even a detached free-style approach to writing I have ever employed or attempted ever before or since. This song was gifted to me because "I" needed a way to express a spiritual connection that was opened to me years ago. The breadth and depth of the meaning of the message and its eloquent natural simplicity of form and style are well beyond my personal abilities. I will *forever* treasure this gift, for this is *Chisum's Song.*

The song is a message. The message is an *acknowledgment* that by being open to it on a personally spiritual level, it makes itself now easily available to me.

It is a message of *connections*; of *holding forever* or *binding eternity to* the seemingly limited sustainability of breaths that we draw in and tears and smiles and therefore meanings of the full range of emotions that we cast outwardly. That what seems limited and perishable across time is actually, in truth, sustained and preserved.

It is a message given in an instinctual language or non-audible perhaps emotional style of communicating that drained the words from my pen, while I merely watched as they were drawn by my hand in a style I yearned was mine. My only involvement was trying to stay out of the way; like dipping my hand into water to get wet, yet trying not to create a single ripple upon the surface, lest I interfere with the message. I tried to be still in the moment as I reflected on the Native American idea: "To pass and leave no trace, like a fish through the water, like a bird in the air."

The message is one of *continuance* and *extension* or *projection*; of one season into and within another; of my limited eyes and sight to its limitless vision and awareness; of the wisdom intrinsic to the wild and nature's true living through the strength of the Spirit given tenderly to the child for the child's growth or evolution or movement through some phase to another.

The message is one of *inter-relatedness* across a broad spectrum of place and time, however on a closely knit family level; that indeed the sea, the land, and the sky are one and that the maker seeks out and cares for his children in this cradle of forever. We are reminded that so connected are all things that the sunrise and the sunset and all held between are *one event*, at *one time*, but with the further understanding that the time, right now, is forever; the infinite within the instant: A concept of a singularity.

If I were you, I'd ask for extraordinary clarification on at least a few things, so for the record: There were no drugs or alcohol or mind altering chemicals of any kind involved that day, that year or years since or before as I don't use them. There were no emotional issues at play in my life or stresses out of the norm. I *was however* yearning to say something; something that I felt was just beyond my capabilities to express and to reach and yet within my ability to grasp, should I be able to reach it. Then, simultaneously with a strong sense of my release or relaxation or opening *it was brought* to me; my role was not to pull in, but to relax and accept; almost the antithesis of writing, more like accepting a gift given with love and with purpose.

9

THE AMBER CRADLE OF FOREVER'S DAY – CHISUM'S SONG

If I could hold forever near,
And breath eternally,
I would grant every breath, every smile-born tear,
Is a gift you've given me.

I search for words n'er penned before,
To quench this parchment soul,
And beseech the Gods of lot and store,
"Guide my hand to their eloquent flow."

The seasons join,
The spirit walks on wings across the sky.
My maker speaks from crimson splendor,
Strong yet tender, eyes so wild and wise.

The sea-born garden of the sun,
Will caress the shore and sigh,
While the meek teach stillness to the strong,
The moon will teach the tide.

To seek the children of the sun,
As they struggle along their way,
For a rising sun, is a setting one,
In The Amber Cradle of Forever's Day.

From love's first blush, and dust to dust,
A rising sun, is a setting one.
You're a piece of the sun, so go shine like one!
In The Amber Cradle of Forever's Day!

THE CRY OF DENALI

I hope you will allow me to cover a fair bit of ground in this one as this song deserves the foundational backdrop that exists before I get into the direct message of the piece itself. Also, by covering points in the next paragraph I want to acknowledge that in writing "Denali" I am not oblivious to the issues that take the forefront when grappling with environmental issues that encompass large pieces of land and therefore many interests of property rights, politics, economics and constitutional issues of Title V and the "Taking Clause" of Eminent Domain. I know my *As I See It* readers out there are sharp, so hang with me.

Often times when I am writing about environmental issues that we face, I refer to our "stewardship" of this or that. To put it in perhaps more blunt terms than some of my friends who are active in animal rights, animal care and environmental concerns commonly do, we people, for better or worse, are the dominant creature of the planet, at least for now. It sounds so ridiculous to say, but this of course means that the odds are that if a condition exists that requires sacrifice between one creature and we people, more often than not, we people will get our way or most of it. This is still the rule although it is tested as the stand fast rule of late, as rather dubious decisions have been made that happen to be in favor of fish or fowl that have had very predictable negative effects that should have tilted the decision in the other direction. I say *dubious* decision here, not because they favored the animals in the immediate, but because the decisions were not made with the context of their long-term overall impact. You see, bad decisions can be made that happen to favor the animals and bad decisions can be made that favor we people. If we are good "stewards" as I intend, we would make the *best* possible decisions concerning our environment taking into account broad implications with real world applications, with actual experts and not politically affiliated yes men, and we would consider also the unintended consequences of our actions or inactions as the case may be before we act. Again, I'm talking real world workable and measureable solutions by fair minded problem solvers as opposed to those who are completely blinded by the dirty duo of ideology and agenda. Our time living here on planet Earth will necessarily be confronted with competing interests. The situation might be how to expand the infrastructure of a growing metropolis, a political issue, while balancing the draw on required tax revenue increases that will be necessary to fund that expansion, both a political, economic and a financial and free market issue. Often business tends to want to outpace infrastructure expansion which is politically palatable when economies are booming. Or in terms of the environment, we may wish to protect a particular species' habitat, but must weigh in very sober terms, any negative impact any land use restrictions would necessarily create as a practical economic matter. These are existential concerns; they are about our continued existence, and as such they require us to envision who we are to be in the future. This vision dictates who we must challenge ourselves to be in the present, and who we are is as much about the decisions we make as it is why we decide as we do, and then how we go about implementing those decisions; for this will be the fulcrum upon which history will judge us; and how exactly do we decide to strike a natural balance.

In "The Cry of Denali," I do not stress the economic issues because they are a *given* in todays world. However, "Denali" does talk to another and I believe extremely crucial facet of the larger decision model. The ecosystem we so often debate is a living creature. It is healthy when it is complete. A complete ecosystem supports healthy life within it, however, when the ecosystem in knocked out of balance for any reason, those who live within it suffer and that includes we folks. In "Denali" I deal with the issue of the needs of ranging predators, in this case wolves, which require large amounts of land to feed and to reproduce in a genetically viable manner that promotes immunity to disease by avoiding inbreeding. I wrote the song for a TV show years ago that I pitched to a major network producer. My pitch was accepted and the idea was that my music would be the backdrop for the story of the reintroduction of the wolf to the Yukon Territory in Alaska. The show had to be scrapped when work moved me west to California and my producer was sent to Russia on assignment (which of course was an extreme disappointment to both of us; maybe someday we can reconvene and complete the circle). I also, however, spoke through the lyric to reach people on a personal level. The chorus says:

> *Cry for the hungry,*
> *Cry for the lonely,*
> *Cry for me only, if I am not free......*

Here and in the verses, I try to show that we all need some semblance of a free habitat; we all need to be seriously considered; we all need to be represented and in an emotionally strong sense that drives home the point that it is not only the animals that we are considering, as if that were not enough, not only all the factors I mentioned in the first paragraph regarding politics and free markets, but our own health within the system, our own sense of connection to the concept of the American wilderness and who we are, the importance we as exceptional Americans place on the natural world and its laws which effected how our constitutional framers created our governing and legal construct and on and on. *Wilderness* is the physical, emotional and spiritual manifestation of a free people.

The title of the song "The Cry of Denali" is made in reference to the cries of the cubs in the den. In researching the wolf population reduction/ eradication, I was shocked at the brutality that was employed. In some cases the wolves had their mouths wired shut so as not to allow them to eat, nor prey, nor communicate nor defend their cubs. In other cases the mothers were simply shot and killed in their dens alongside their cubs, who were allowed to live, but only defenseless against attack and not yet able to hunt for themselves. The cubs were doomed to a horrible death.

14

So the cries I'm speaking of in "Denali" are the innocent cries of those whose only desire is to be as they are, to be accepted. If we are wise, they are to be nurtured as part of a healthy balanced ecosystem. The cries of Denali cry out to the horror we inflict that has its origin in our ignorance. The cries of Denali cry out to the better parts of ourselves to replace ignorance and therefore fear with knowledge and understanding and therefore compassion, and to replace violence with coexistence, to replace death with life; all this, not surprisingly, "from the mouths of babes." So as I say in the song:

"In a fight for survival, a song of compassion for the children of the land and the sea, in the Cry of Denali..."

The true struggle for survival is not in conquering more land and more control, but more of a struggle to conquer our own fear and ignorance, for they are the true forebears of the tyrant of hate, violence and hurt; while knowledge and understanding is the key to our futures.

All too often we think of the howls of wolves as sounding so very primal. Perhaps in this case the more *fundamental*, indeed the more *primal* vocabulary is the best one to communicate to us, that all those wolves ask of us, is to allow them to be as they were intended to be, and to play a role we are only beginning to understand. In this way, we have come to Denali to seek our teacher and to learn; once again, what is our place in this sanctuary of freedom.

"Wilderness" is a state of mind and a state of being that is part of who we are as Americans, and as Americans, we should do no less than understand ALL of the implications of environmental decisions, and we should never avoid or diminish the understanding of ourselves as a free people. How we see and how we treat the wilderness and the creatures that thrive within it, are how we will ultimately see and how we will ultimately treat each other in the long run. In that regard it is a truly difficult decision; in that regard it is essential that we get the balance right; in that regard it's a good thing that Americans are making

15

the decision. Who better to make the hard call when freedom needs to be defended than we outdoor loving Americans? "The Cry of Denali" is a cry out for freedom. We as Americans are uniquely qualified to understand the implications here and therefore to assign the proper weight to its defense.

THE CRY OF DENALI

You can read the stories cast across the northern skies
And hold the spirits captive in the gaze of steely eyes
A shimmer of majesty, there's silver in the snow
I've come to find the secrets you have come to know

Of living lives with pride, warm hearts against the cold
I've come to find you here; I've come to find my soul
Sometimes it seems we live in worlds so far apart
In truth the hunter lives here deep within our hearts

Yet we, cry for the hungry, cry for the lonely.
Cry for me only, if I am not free.
To see with your vision, to live with your courage.
Your cry out to the spirit in me.
In The Cry of Denali!

And so it's not so strange that I've come unto your land
I've come to hear your song, I've come to understand
I've come to realize there are things I need to know
I've come to find the truth, in truth, I've come to grow

I seek compassion in a cold and desperate time
I seek my family and I wish that you were mine
The student waits now patiently upon the rise
For the wind has changed and now the master has arrived

And we, cry for the hungry, cry for the lonely.
We cry for the children, of the land and the sea.
We see with your vision, we live with your courage.
As you cry out to the spirit in me.
In The Cry of Denali !

I've found compassion in these cold and desperate times
I've found my family, and I know that you are mine
We walk together now, with passion and with grace
And live in harmony within your sacred place

To cry for the hungry, cry for the lonely.
To cry for the children, for they must be free.
To see with your vision, to live with your courage.
All this you give now to me.
In the Cry of Denali !

In a fight for survival, a song of compassion.
For the children of the land and the sea.
In The Cry of Denali !
In The Cry of Denali !
In The Cry_____!
In The Cry of Denali.

CANDLELIGHT AND WINE

"Candlelight and Wine" is a love song that was written in a dream. When I awoke one morning years ago, the song flowed from my hand in a single series of natural strokes of the pen. It was the expression of the power and elegance of the deepness and richness of true love for another person. It is a song devoid of any manipulation whatsoever. "Who taught the sunrise of fire and light, and who made the moon glow to romance the night?" The author of the miracle of Nature's creation in all its awe and splendor is the author of the power of love itself. That which created all we see, taste and hear is the author of how we act, and think and feel. It seems fitting that the setting is an intimate one. Two lovers for a moment sharing their love for one another as if they are, at that minute, all that there is, so captive they are in the eyes and hearts and spirit of the other, through the glow of a single flame.

CANDLELIGHT AND WINE

A table for two, on one magic night
One flickering candle, will dance in your eyes
Few words are spoken, but hearts will speak clear
And I'm here in paradise, whenever you are near

Candlelight and Wine, and the music in your eyes
Harmonies and rhymes, and a medley of your sighs
This gift you give to me, is the wonder of the dream I live in,
And I'll share it now with you, Candlelight and Wine.

Who taught the sunrise, of fire and light?
And who made the moon glow, to romance the night?
Who stole the canyons, away from the sea?
And who brought this miracle of your love to me?

Candlelight and Wine, and the music in your eyes
Harmonies and rhymes, and a medley of gentle sighs
This gift you give to me, is the wonder of the love I live in
And I'll share it now with you, Candlelight and Wine.

Candlelight and Wine, and the music in your eyes
Harmonies and rhymes, and a medley of gentle sighs
This gift you give to me, is the wonder of the dream I live in
And before this night is through,
I will pour myself on you,
Tonight this love will shine, through Candlelight and Wine.

Eagles Over Aberdeen

The story of the eagles at Aberdeen is a local story with global implications. A story at once of discovery, resurgence and of rebirth. The discovery of a single nesting pair of eagles, the resurgence of their endangered population and the rebirth of the ideal that we must protect wild things in wild places.

A story that began in the mid-1970's at a U. S. Army proving grounds in Maryland, when a single nesting pair of eagles was spotted. A scant few more were later identified on the 75,000 acre facility of woods and marshes along the Chesapeake Bay that is the Aberdeen Proving Grounds, some 35 miles northeast of Baltimore. The population of eagles across the nation had been decimated by the reduction of sustainable habitat and the pervasive use of pesticides. The pesticide runoff entered the waters where the eagles would fish and when ingested would render any future eggs too soft to support the weight of the nesting mother in the nest. All this left the eagles relegated to the Endangered Species List as their numbers moved toward extinction. The eagles' homes were dwindling and their babies were dying. The testing of the explosives by the Army at the gunnery testing range would often ignite wildfires that would further threaten the nesting pair. However, the civilian contractors and Army personnel, who I call the "kindred spirits" of the eagles at Aberdeen, would not allow any harm to come to the aerie. It would be here that a stand would be taken to defend and insure the future of these eagles. At this Department of Defense facility, dedicated to testing the tools our brave men and women in uniform use in the defense of our country, the people there then further committed themselves to defending these eagles. As our forefathers fought to create a free society in a sovereign country, as our

21

troops fight today to defend her, so too these fine people fought to preserve the future of the very embodying symbol of American pride and freedom. And defend they did! Due to the resilience of the eagles and the compassion of those civilian and military personnel, Aberdeen now boasts a population of over 300 eagles, the largest concentration of eagles in any one location in the state.

This song was born of that experience. A story of resurgence that should be played out all across this great nation and everywhere wild creatures yearn to live free: A lesson that we must do everything in our power as guardians of their futures. An acknowledgement and a solemn vow that under our stewardship of the environment we must protect wild things in wild places and the ecosystems and habitat upon which they rely......" Eagles over Aberdeen forever you will fly!"

EAGLES OVER ABERDEEN

Centuries ago they dared to take a stand
With a vision for the future of this land
Freedom born on the shores of a new world
And carried to the sky by your wings as flags unfurled
They would be free, but not on bended knees
They would do all they could, to be all they could be

You embody the spirit of their fight
And guard this flickering candle on windy nights
Golden wings spread o'er a promised land
Within you lies the spirit we understand
The spirit of America lives in your eyes
You still move me to tears, when you fly

And Eagles over Aberdeen still grace my Maryland skies
And here out over Aberdeen I still hear freedom's cry
Of all the wonders I've ever seen, I've never seen
The grace of your dance in the sky
And Eagles over Aberdeen forever you will fly!

Today the struggle is harder to understand
When the suffering we see is brought by our own hands
Rachel warned of the "Silent Springs" to come
And freedom's sanctuary on the run
When poisoned minds bring poison to our young
Another kind of battle must be won

Once again we will dare to take this stand
To forever preserve your future in this land
Freedom now reborn on Maryland shores
Will inspire hearts and minds to reach for more
This proving ground has kept our nation strong
Let it test our will forever, to hear your song

And Eagles over Aberdeen will grace our nation's skies
Forever over Aberdeen we'll still hear freedom's cry
For all the wonders our children see, as you fly free
To carry their dreams to the sky
Eagles over Aberdeen forever you will fly!

And Eagles over Aberdeen will grace our Maryland skies
And here out over Aberdeen we'll still hear freedom's cry
Of all the wonders I've ever seen, I've never seen
The grace of your dance in the sky!
And Eagles over Aberdeen forever you will fly!
Eagles over Aberdeen forever you will fly!

GIVE ME YOUR SONG

A song is such an organic and elegant thing of beauty. Born from the spirit of being, filtered through the experience of a single individual, molded and tempered as it grows towards its crescendo and yes worn and frayed from the very experience of it all; a true exemplar of the experience of life. No wonder why it is the vehicle most used to evoke so many emotions with which we are all so very familiar.

"Give Me Your Song" is actually asking quite a great deal from another. It grants acceptance but asks at the same time for the trust of another to be accepted fully and completely without condition; each a gifted singer in search of their natural song that has been born in the heart of another; An acknowledgement that one was meant to be in order for another to be complete or at least fulfilled. In this relationship we can clearly see the enormous value of each individual person. We are each valuable to ourselves and integral, perhaps even indispensable to the lives of another.

You, the reader of this book or perhaps my listener, are enormously valuable to me. What I write, what I sing or say would have no place to be, if not for you.

GIVE ME YOUR SONG

All of this time, all of these fears
All of my life, all of these tears
All of these songs, with so much to say
Still the words get in my way.

Show me a sign, show me a light
Guide me back home, through this dark night
I've been away, for far too long
Grant me this peace, Give Me Your Song.

I know you feel it too
The love between us is right
But if this love plays us for fools
"Let fortune favor the foolish" hearts tonight.

There is a place, where true love thrives
On wings of grace, that reach for the sky
Where broken hearts heal, and spirits grow strong
A rebirth of life that's waited too long.

I've found that place, deep in your eyes
Honest and true, gentle and wise
Two weary hearts, together so strong
Grant me this peace, Give Me Your Song.

All of the things, I want to do
All of my plans, I've made them for you
Though we've just met, I've known you so long
You live in my heart, you are my song.
Grant me this peace, Give Me Your Song.

You Are the Spirit in Me

As the sun slips down through the branches of the trees and the infinite universe of stars and space reveal themselves, it's natural to, at once, feel enormously moved in knowing that each of us is a part of all the grandeur that we see, and yet, feel rather small and perhaps even a bit insignificant given the enormity of it all. But we need not feel insignificant for long, because the stars teach us that they are islands of shimmering life giving light, in every measurable sense, very much like the sun that just escaped capture by the trees on our western horizon. Indeed that very tree is reaching, branches extended, towards one of the two sources of its life-giving creations; holding dearly to Mother Earth while reaching for the sun.

This concept of an element that exists outside of the physical realm that is just as real and just as vital to being as anything we can touch and feel was the inspiration for "You Are The Spirit In Me." The energy given by the sun makes all the wonders of a living Earth switch on and keeps them thriving, growing and evolving as we all fly through the vastness of the universe held to the ground by another force we cannot touch, feel or see, called gravity. This is still another bit of evidence among many such not so subtle hints that we are more than what meets the eye. It is also evidence that we are, each of us, capable of doing rather grand things if we keep in mind all the wonderful and powerful forces that saw fit to give us a chance to be.

We should also learn and stay keenly aware that we need each other not just in physical body but also in spirit, in heart and in the soul. The invisible hand that guides the stars through the sky, is the same hand that brings hearts and minds together in the celebration of the self, and the celebration of being part of another. It is a lesson in being aware of the context of being part of a living and breathing universe that looks back upon itself through the infinite vastness of space all the while falling in love as we answer the question, "Am I alone?" The answer of course shines as brightly in the stars so far away above as it does in your lovers eyes just beside you; "Of course you are not alone!" In fact, you are never truly alone.

You Are the Spirit in Me

The sun has fallen through the trees
The stars are dancing through eternity
Within this endless darkened sky
Their light and magic burning deep inside

And it occurred to me, a hand that I can't see
Has guided them for so long
Oh and could it be, just as with you and me
It's your heart in mine, baby that makes me strong

You are the fire in my eyes
You are the pleasure in my sighs
You are the passion in my kiss
You are so much more than this

You're my heart's rhythm, my life's rhyme
For what is meter without time?
You are the place my love light shines
You Are the Spirit in Me!

This is a dance between two souls
Within a world that's growing dark and cold
But in the beat of every heart
There's just no way of telling us apart

And it occurred to me, is this our destiny?
We have been fighting too long
Oh and could it be, just as with you and me
Only together can our hearts beat strong!

I hear the echo of my soul
When your heart's thunder starts to roll
A simple truth that we can hold
You Are the Spirit in Me!

And with this vision we have sight
With your compassion bring me light
You are what guides me through the night
You Are the Spirit in Me!

You are the fire in my eyes
You are the pleasure in my sighs
You bring the passion to my kiss
You are so much more than this

And with this vision we have sight
With your compassion bring me light
Come now and guide me through this night
You Are the Spirit in Me!
You Are the Spirit in Me!
You are the Spirit!
You Are the Spirit in Me!

HERE'S TO YOU

For anyone who has ever had the misfortune to experience the gut wrenching pain of feeling that the future may be hopeless or even for a moment felt an abject poverty of self-worth, this song is an expression of thanks in its most simple if not most poignant form. A thank you to another for being there, in whatever way was needed to lift another from the depths and shadows in which we can sometimes find ourselves. It is also a reminder to each of us of the power we have to help another find their way, by looking to us as an example perhaps, that tough times befall all of us and that the darkness is not your destiny. That adversity is the stone upon which we will sharpen our skills and temper our spirit. A bold statement that life is inherently worth living and that we each have inherent value to ourselves and can pass that on to another that has lost their way. We can each be examples that the way we live and the effect we have on others along the way defines us and secures our humanity and sense of self-worth. "So here's to those with the courage."

HERE'S TO YOU

There was a time, when I was so lost
No direction and nothing to share.
The fear in my heart, almost tore me apart
I quit trying, I just didn't dare.

Though you were there beside me,
I was sure it would scare you away.
To see my self-doubt as too high a price to pay.

But somehow you managed to turn me around,
You saw more in me than I ever knew.
How blessed are we, who find in another,
A someone to live up to.

I'm not sure where it's going,
But I'm sure my life isn't the same.
It's not winning or losing, but loving to play the game.

So, here's those with the courage,
Who dare to say dreams can come true.
For they make the world a better place.
And my darling Here's to You.
For you've made my world a better place,
My darling Here's to You.

WHERE WORDS DON'T COME EASY

I firmly believe that most people have kind hearts and good intentions in their dealings with others. I also believe however that the stresses and strains life places upon us, and more significantly, the stresses we create and place upon ourselves, have us act in ways we would rather not act, and hear our own voices give tirades we wish were never spoken at all.

We often show the uncanny ability to achieve exactly those outcomes we espouse vehemently to hold in the deepest contempt when it comes to being the captains of our own futures. We place ourselves in situations that are so miserable or at least so undesirable, that when we are fortunate enough to extricate ourselves from them, we immediately do two things; first we swear we will never, EVER, repeat the steps which gave rise to the situation EVER again, and second we get on about repeating those exact transgressions once again.

Chalk it up to being creatures of habit? Well, maybe I suppose. Then again, perhaps some habits are really better off being broken, lest they become tradition.

WHERE WORDS DON'T COME EASY

A few years ago in the perfect dress
For better, for worse, or more or less
It was all they had but they vowed their best to each other.

But just last night in the crime of crimes
And without warning love turned on a dime
They're both victims but they'll do time together.

Here, Where Words Don't Come Easy
Hearts are left alone to wonder how a true love died
And here, lovers pay dearly
For the cost of their admission
With insatiable ambition
And love that's starved for time
Where Words Don't Come Easy.

Now words can be weapons as well as tools
Have you never had a loaded question aimed at you?
Pointed as arrows and hardened like steel
To target a heart that may never heal.

So enter a wise man among the fools
A master of the game is but a slave to the rules
For when time is running short, we're all left stranded.

Here, Where Words Don't Come Easy
Careless words are left out on a cold and bitter wind
And here, we all pay dearly
When messages we send
Make enemies of friends
That won't be back again
Where Words Don't Come Easy.

It's a place where we've all been,
And swear we won't go back again,
Though we, don't know how we got in anyway.

But tender words were left unspoken,
And what was done left good hearts broken,
Regret is but the hollow token we'll pay.

It's something we've known for so very long
When the pace is fast, when the race is long
When confused voices would steer you wrong
To your heart be true, to your love be strong.

For outside the winds of change still roar
They'll cry out for you, and you'll crave for more
With the strangest feeling you've been here before
And you know too well, who's at your door.

Here, Where Words Don't Come Easy
We walk away from love we called our own
And here, we all pay dearly
For things we should have known
When we stray too far from home
We'll find out on our own
Where Words Don't Come Easy.

ONLY FOR YOU

I want for you all the promise that the future brings and that all your dreams to come true. Pretty simple thought, right? I thought about that when I asked myself, what would I wish if there was one thing I could wish for someone I love? If I had one bite out of the apple as they say, to make that one wish. Well, for me, being the gluttonous type, I thought "I'd wish for it all, and why not? It was Dr. Carl Sagan himself who said we are all made of 'star stuff,' so we are made of bits and pieces of everything, why not ask for everything?"

Oh and it's just a little play on words when I say, "I want this only for you." I simply mean, that this is the *only thing* I want for you....simply, all of it, everything you can dream! So I say this with my tongue firmly planted in my cheek.

The album that "Only for You" was part of was my first visit to the recording studio on my personal little budget. I was recording a collection of songs wherein I wanted to show people in the industry that I could write across the spectrum of musical genres and lo and behold I could carry a tune in a bucket if handed one. "Only for You" was the answer to the collection that needed an uptempo light-hearted song and in my constant attempts at doing everything I do a little differently than that which has come before, my intent was to make the song sound like a live performance might sound. All too often music can become antiseptic and clinical in the studio. So when all the buttons and knobs where turned and tuned in the exactly proper positions to record this song, I said "move em all around a bit and hit record." Honestly, I don't know why some people even put up with me at all! But let's move on. I don't want to think about that too long!

37

ONLY FOR YOU

Come close, let me hold you
And tell you of a world I want for you.
The promise that the future brings
Can make the songs we sing come true.
I want this only, Only for You.

Cool nights, warm hands
Clear water on white sand and foam too.
A sea to cast your dreams upon
And stars to guide a lifetime through.
I want this only, Only for You.
I want this only, only this for you.

Is it too much what I ask for you?
Too much to think you might feel the way I do?
One shining world bright and new!
Where all of our dreams, all of our dreams can come true.
Only, Only for You.
Only, Only for You.

Wide-eyed baby's wonder
The spell I've fallen under sees me through.
A lullaby within your sigh
And gray skies fade to blue.
I want this only, Only for You.
I want this only, and only this, for you.

Is it too much what I ask for you?
Too much to think you might feel the way I do?
One shining world bright and new!
Where all of our dreams, all of our dreams can come true.
Only, Only for You.
Only, Only for You.
Only, Only for You.
Only, all of this for you.

YOU TAUGHT US TO FLY

That Which Endures

A Reflection on the Timeless Legacy of Mr. John Denver

Words matter. Not merely as tools for the conveyance of a thought, rather, and more importantly, they are the life giving breath of passion that lives within an idea and touches us when they are spoken or sung. One of my favorite words is "aspire." I've always felt that John Denver's music is as aspirational as it is inspirational and introspective. Indeed, what attracted me quite naturally to his music, in addition to nature's metaphors and the celebration and defense of our natural treasures and splendor for which he became known, is a message that challenges each of us to grow; inwardly and outwardly. I have always believed in the importance of being aware of and nurturing ones' own gifts and sharing them for the good of all and to the benefit of each. To give, and yes to receive, always with grace, and all the while striving as I say "to be more when tomorrow's sun rises than what we were when yesterday's sun came to rest."

A true American troubadour, Mr. Denver's gift to us was to blend his message to songs only he could create; songs only he could sing. Once named "Seize the Eagle" by Native Americans who understood keenly the spirit that sang out in such glory from deep within this man's soul.

I have been singing for as long as I can remember and writing for a bit less than that. And while my influences, musically and otherwise are broad, I am fortunate to have been touched by this once-in-a-generation talent; this once-in-a-lifetime gift to us all. His message, his energy and his singular ability to reach so many diverse people and indeed diverse cultures has and always will transcend the ages. In joy, it will forever echo across space and time as an eloquent and wise reminder that we are all brothers and sisters on this beautiful garden hurling through the heavens, children of the sun, celebrating it all.

So it is with gratitude and respect that I say to "Seize the Eagle," thank you John.

Forever, I wish you Peace.

Chris Mentch

YOU TAUGHT US TO FLY

(A Tribute to Mr. John Denver)

Too soon.
Why must legends leave us always too soon?
They bring reason and rhymes to our desperate times,
And harmony to a world so out of tune.

Tell me why.
For my life, I can't understand why,
In a world that cries out for their vision and sight,
Their wisdom and light on the darkest of nights,
Must the brightest stars fall from the sky?

Goodbye.
Never had a chance to say goodbye,
Or to thank you for all that you've given me.
"Seize the Eagle" taught us to be free!
To be more than we are, and all we can be…I will not say goodbye!

So for all those who love you,
And all who believe in you,
Your message will never die.
You Taught Us to Fly!

WE ARE ONE

"We Are One" was my first original song and my first song recorded in a recording studio. Written and recorded in Baltimore Maryland, "We Are One" is a critical examination of what I believe is our perception of our role as cohabitants of the planet. Now I know, I know, stay with me, I'm not going pie in the sky and becoming philosophically derailed on you but I think it's certainly a topic worth consideration since we think ourselves fairly important to it all.

I am only humbly submitting for consideration in this song that while it's a great thing for each of us as individuals to find our own personal center to help us balance the various aspects of our lives, it's best not to consider ourselves generally as the center of everything else outside of ourselves. Put another way, to play our part at its best, we must understand our role in the broad scheme as best we can. It is in this way that we can indeed have the most positive effect on our world generally and in each other's lives individually. We can be a force to make things better than they would be had we all not been around for a while, but we have to have context and perspective.

When I say "in the innocent eyes of the wild and the young," I am referring to the innocence of all creatures, we humans and animals alike, who in our youthful time open our eyes to a world we have yet to explore or understand or even to affect. I am ever mindful that the best test of any society is the manner it treats the least, or the most vulnerable among them. That it is not necessary to fully understand that which you grant the treasure of one's compassion nor is it the measure of a creatures intellect that governs exactly how much compassion it deserves. We as a people are only worthy of this life in the equal measure that we value, defend, embrace, nurture and share it. Sound familiar?

In my mind a truly beautiful woman or man is one who embodies equal amounts of courage, compassion, spirit and understanding for they tend to exhibit the empathy that we all as evolving persons will come to understand extoll our values, define our humanity and secure our destiny. For "We Are One."

WE ARE ONE

Light-years ago we saw the promise
In a world free from hunger, free from pain
With all the time that's now slipped through our hands
Are we any closer to that day?

Do we really need to see the children crying?
Do we really want to feel their mother's pain?
And, are the choices not right in front of us?
Will we do nothing again?

We must understand the challenge lies before us
In a stewardship of life forever run
We are guardians of all of our children's dreams
And all that live beneath a golden sun

Oh, We Are One
Oh, We Are One

We take our place on life's stage front and center
Superior in purpose and design
We disregard a renaissance of wisdom
But arrogance can't stand the test of time

For there's a message in the life that surrounds us
In voices that fall silent to the gun
In the cry of the eagle, the song of the whale
It lies in the eyes of our young

Oh, We Are One
Oh, We Are One

For all of us, a matter of survival
By each of us, so much more could be done
But our first steps will signal the arrival
Of a new age just begun!

To live our lives with courage and compassion
To care for those we don't yet understand
We seek out and embrace our new family
In the sea, air, and on the land

For there's a message in the life that surrounds us
That must not be laid silent by the gun
In the cry of the eagle, the song of the whale
It shines in the eyes, of our young
The innocent eyes, of the wild and the young

Oh, We Are One
Oh, We Are One
Oh, We Are One

POETRY IS

Poetry is a feast for the senses and words are the ingredients that tempt the yearning palate.

Poetry gives words purpose, and when words have purpose, truth can be told. Hearts and minds can be reached by their inherent purity and authenticity: A message not poisoned or tortured by contrived manipulation but rather born naturally of true experience, openly accepted by appealing to a sense of natural dignity and grace of our common experiences, both in sorrow, and in rapture.

It is here that we can all dine in delight on the treasures of the spirit upon life's bountiful table, tempted by her splendid variation of themes, perfectly presented to fulfill, enrich and satisfy every longing hunger and nurture the soul.

She wishes us *bon appétit!* — Chris

Poems Table of Contents

A Living Peace

I am the son of an American soldier. A warrior of the U.S. Army infantry and a well decorated one at that, my father having earned three Bronze Stars for acts of valor during combat. Indeed my father, a career military man, retired a Chief Warrant Officer (CW3) in the non-commissioned ranks. In this regard I believe that I am, while certainly not *the most qualified* person to speak of the value of peace, certainly one *uniquely qualified* to speak on the topic as roughly only one percent of the American population currently serve in the armed forces and therefore the same percentage of American family members currently deal with the realities of military life.

America, this beautiful America, is the most powerful yet the most benevolent country on the planet. Its warriors fight not necessarily out of hatred for any particular enemy, but out of love of country and family and peace. The American soldier fights at the tip of the spear defending America's innocents from the most evil and pernicious enemies ever devised by the darkest villains history has ever brought forth. The American warrior stands at once as the most formidable and lethal fighting man and woman and yet the most caring and compassionate soul that has ever existed in the fire and fog on the battlefield. The American warrior and their families are the most peace loving persons among us. I am as grateful for every American warrior and their families as I am my next breath.

What I try to say in "A Living Peace" is that peace is a way of being and a way of living. Peace must be nurtured as well as defended, here at home and abroad. If it is true about politics, that it exists as a vehicle to replace violence as a mechanism of social change, than surely peace itself is the vital lifeblood that allows a nation to evolve to the elegant facets of life; the great discoveries of medicine and science, the great advances in engineering and art, and the great strides of exploring our universe. Peace allows us both the launch pad and the launch vehicle to rise both literally and figuratively for the stars and ask the grand cosmic questions of "Why are we here?" and, "What is our purpose?" and, "Are we alone?"

So peace is the condition precedent to the advancement of the family of man; and peace is a condition of love. From this proud son of a great American warrior, dear reader, dear listener, I wish you "A Living Peace"

A LIVING PEACE

If there is one thought that we should hold so very dear,
one moment to seek and sustain.
If there is one ideal that should guide how we choose to live our lives.
If there is one guiding principle upon which we will chart the course
for our posterity.
It could not be more clear.

If there is one moment of sudden clarity,
where the true nature of things are revealed.
It is in that epiphany of rapture of grace and of joy,
that we will at long last find.
That all that we need or ever needed,
is held deeply within us where it has been all that time.

If there is but one common bond within this life,
one rhythm that beats within each heart,
one message carried aloft upon windswept whispers.
It could not be more true.

If there is one aspiration of the human soul,
one reason to be, and to live.
If there is but one worthy destiny for us all.
It could not be more solemn.

Let us then, hold closely that thought.
Let us defend that ideal.
Let us trust that principle.
And let forever live within that moment.

Let us strengthen that bond.
Let our hearts pound out the rhythm.
Let us sing with glory and pride.
Let us aspire to seek the destiny that awaits those who make that
solemn vow.
And let us all commit ourselves to it now.

Let there be Peace Upon This Earth.
Let the fire not consume, but bring us light.
Let us gather together within it's glow.
Like the stars that once seemed so very far away,
that warm our spirits now in their radiant rebirth, tonight.

For if there is to be that brave new world.
If we are to realize that Grand Vision.
If it is indeed Peace that we seek.
We must look first deep within.

For it is there that shadows cling as phantom chains to the darkness.
For it is there where the shackles are slipped by the quickening light.
It is there the feckless yoke of the tyrant yields to the will of the
prisoner,
whose faith holds the key to the groaning dungeons of doubt.

For Peace is not merely a condition we seek.
Nor is it the elusive egalitarian master that exists merely to frustrate us,
as we struggle to find our proper place, and practice and way.
It may be with or without conflict but is always a sister to justice,
and forever the sanctuary for the free soul.

She lives not to service pens drained in anger, hubris or hate,
but to those whose alliteration's are sacrosanct and
guided by the invisible passion through the pages of life.
A thirst only quenched by the wisdom of the ages,
and sealed by the imprimatur of the sovereign.

Behold now Peace:
She is forever a way of living.
She is forever the garden of love.
Peace is the ultimate teacher,
of how to embrace the lessons of this earth,
and still reach for the stars above.

Peace is the giver of promise,
granting a space for hope to survive.
She is the giver of all that has come before.
She is the vision that keeps the future alive.

A singularity of the infinite splendor.
To each of the many she is the only one.
Yes Peace is A Way of Living.
And on this day, A Living Peace, has begun.

...Pax vobiscum! Hoc erat in votis.
...(Peace be with you! This was among my prayers.)

YESTERDAY'S EYES – LADY HISTORY

We are so often told that those who do not learn the lessons of history are doomed to repeat the mistakes of the past. I think the cyclical machinations of the fashion industry prove this axiom quite well. It seems to keep correcting itself. Will we wear peg legged pants or bell-bottoms or something in between? Can we just pick one already till they have a chance wear out? Oh, and I love the line in the ABBA song "Waterloo," that "The history book on the shelf, is always repeating itself." I can hear the cheers and jeers of ABBA fans and non-fans alike, but the point is made well and the title "Waterloo" is perfect. But "Waterloo" may not have any meaning to the listener if they do not have even a cursory knowledge of history.

We are creatures of habit and we all know it, so it astounds me why we do not teach it more thoroughly in our schools. History is life's *on the job training of the generations* and we should be much more mindful of her lessons and the lessons of our elders still with us might I add. Their experiences and their wisdom are treasures for each generation that follows so let's all wise up and listen up to the voices of yesterday that whisper to us of what we can expect, and perhaps even plan for, tomorrow.

Yesterday's Eyes – Lady History

It's said that "history seldom discloses it's alternatives".
And indeed one can never discern with exacting clarity
If it was wisdom that may have saved us,
Or simply fate when it betrays us

Yet there is a teacher and a sage, of that yet to be
And through Yesterdays Eyes we will follow our fine guide
And walk deliberately, with Lady History.

She is kind to all of her students
She disciplines the forgetful
She teaches the self-aware
She rewards the tenacious
Listen to her
Watch her
And treasure her intuition.

FEAR NOT, THE NIGHT

Seeking understanding is at its core, in my opinion a foundational underpinning of compassion. We need not yet have understood someone, to be compassionate to him or her, but we must be seeking to understand them. I believe that being compassionate is an act of *self preservation*; therefore not merely an act done for the benefit of another, although we can hope that was its primary intent. In this way, by being compassionate and understanding in our nature we can learn about another, about ourselves and indeed about our world.

In "Fear Not, The Night" I focus on the example of how when one of our senses is taken from us, the other senses fill the void by becoming more acute and versatile in their sensitivity, application and function. They "up their game" to do whatever needs to be done to replace at least in part that missing element of taking in the world that we have lost. This is an example of how we are actually hard wired to be explorers and to understand. How wonderful a thought that we are all both the curious type as well as the kind and understanding type, and what that may portend for the world we share and our combined futures.

In the piece I put forth that when darkness steals our sight, our capacity to hear more acutely takes over. Hearing steps in front of fearing. Understanding steps in front of closing up. In this way we grow and the silent whisper of learning saves us from the tyrant of fear.

Again, I hope you can see that how we treat others and how we treat the world around us has a direct impact on the future we will experience for ourselves. So while we all can hope we are compassionate and understanding as acts of kindness, we can also celebrate the fact that once in a while we can splurge and at the same time do something for ourselves.

FEAR NOT, THE NIGHT

When the darkness steals our sight,
We listen more closely.
When we listen more closely, we learn.
When we learn, we grow.
When we grow, we understand.
That when the darkness steals our sight,
Silent wisdom whispers,
"Fear Not, the Night."

This Letter That I Have Found

Many things are thoroughly and completely true and I have no idea why. One of those things is why, when I want to get really comfortable, I begin some ritualistic quest to seek out the most torn and tattered forms of clothing imaginable. In fact, the most comfortable ones can barely boast to remain items of actual clothing at all. No one in their right mind, so I guess that immediately excludes your humble author, would choose to wrap themselves publically or privately in these articles of thread remainders which barely actually exist at all; only at a level one measurement above the molecular hurdle. The color has been stripped away and the form has been wiped out. The seams gave up their battle long ago and that was even before large pieces de-evolved into airborne fuzz that flies around for a while before landing somewhere only to be used by a spider for who knows what. I don't know why all of this is, but it is and I and the *"used-to-be-a-shirt"* shirt I am currently wearing agree.

Maybe it's because it acts as a reminder of the simpler days when I was just a boy. My normal everyday outfit was an ensemble of grass stained tennis shoes with laces that got shorter and shorter because they snapped about every two weeks and somehow I still managed to retain them as my originals by altering their path through or around the lace holes until I had enough left at my finger tips to tie something resembling a knot. My pants, jean cutoff shorts, the official gear of the time, again tissue paper thin from washes numbering in the tens of thousands with random ventilation areas where only super thin white horizontal threads remain as a testament to the endurance of Levi Strauss products. The shirt, a tank top, and out the door.

In "This Letter That I Have Found" I tried to explore this condition from the viewpoint of the shirt itself, that years ago was placed in an old chest which would play the role of the shirt's time capsule. Like any time capsule worth its salt, the shirt is accompanied by a letter that acts as the shirts voice to the reader. As I wrote the poem, the largest share of it in one draft without correction or changes, I realized more deeply what we all know; that while the "things" we take through our lives with us hold some type of reminder of some event or some feeling, some victory or defeat, some lesson or love of years past, that they are also mooring devices that can actually help ground us in the current day. They take us back so viscerally that we can more than just remember past times but we can almost taste the air of fresh cut grass, feel the thrill of youthful exuberance often and most wisely at the simplest of things, and remember approaching each new day with the energy of a stallion whose muscles quiver and twitch seconds before launching out of the gate to win the Triple Crown. It amazes me how incredibly powerful the mind is, and how these inanimate objects act as beacons back home or like a trail of breadcrumbs there so we can trace our steps back to a place where we saw the world with less jaded eyes, with hearts not only open to love but seeking it out in whatever form it was blessed upon us. A place in our lives where it was not just an interesting hobby to attempt to create something but we created monster bicycles and dynasty pick-up Pro Bowl-quality football teams whose playbooks consisted of scratches in the dirt that would show the receiver the route through the little pebbles that were the steel curtain defense and the local bullies' secondary. This, my friends, is the magical stuff. There is, mercifully so, no iPhone app for that.

To further prove the magic of all of this the shirt reveals that it has known of the boys life aspirations and the dreams of the boy, for the dreams told the shirt so, when they too were closed within the time capsule chest kept warm by the boy's tattered shirt. Indeed the boy's dreams had watched the boy through the years and watched him grow through triumph and pain, and his dreams, with the shirt, knew that the boy would return one day looking down at them this time through a man's eyes.

By the end of the poem we find that after all these years the adult had not been stripped of his boyish love of life. However, this time it was the body of the once youthful boy that was more tattered and worn, but yet wiser for the effort and strife. So valuable is this realization that the man once again, keeps the old shirt, holds dear to his new found realization that he is doing quite well thank you, and vows to return to the chest once again in the years to come to walk through this passage, this learning, this experience, this life.

THIS LETTER THAT I HAVE FOUND

I rescued a letter that I buried away,
In the bottom of a drawer, at the end of some day.
It's been years since I laid that correspondence to rest.
But it would be the search for one old shirt,
That brought me back to that chest.

Lying buried and silent in her patient repose.
Yesterday's reminder of what today I should know.
For we often forget, we are wiser than we think.
Assuming that with time, wisdom will save us from the brink.

The shirt is worn and tired, but it still fits just fine,
Lending meaning to being yours, and you being mine.
Yes the shirt still fits after all of these nights,
Warm as the laughter and torn from the fights.

So I'll lay my weary head back down,
Wrapped in a dear friend that brought me around,
Once again, to a letter that I've found.
And it read,

> *"I am your yesterday can you remember me now?*
> *I've waited to be found again, and I hoped that somehow,*
> *That this shirt would still tug at the threads of your heart.*
> *As the life that you weave, might bring you back to the start."*

"I'm the son of your hand, and what you've waited to say,
Just one footprint in the sand, from so far away.
I've kept my true vigil here frozen in time,
Awaiting a restless young man, with his weary mind."

"You see your dreams have been waiting; yes they knew you would come.
Watching you cautiously walking, and watching you run.
They where here when you laid me down softly to rest
Kept warm and safe huddled by this shirt in this chest."

"They told me something very long ago,
Something today that I think you should know.
That all you were seeking was there all the time,
All that you hoped that someday you'd find."

"The person that you so wanted to be
With the wisdom to know, that life is more than we see.
To someday find comfort somewhere on your way
And that all of your searching would find you today."

"And so now here you are, from the end to the start.
A man of time's teachers, still a young boy at heart.
Welcome home son, it's been quite a journey and yet
You were never too far away and, never one to forget."

"The persistence of memory, has been your kind friend,
And now it's become time, to lay me down again.
Now I'll watch this man labor, and I'll watch this boy play
And as the years grow late, I'll be found again someday."

"It's nice to see the shirt of a boy, can still fit a man fine
And that life's lessons and scars did not leave the child behind.
For only a child's eyes could clearly see
That today will be yesteryear, when you next rescue me."

And the letter still sits, after all of this time,
Under a shirt that somehow, still fits just fine.
For the shirt is a companion and to this vow I am bound,
Lay me down, but don't forget me.
And This Letter That I Have Found.

THE RISK PERCEIVED (THE THINGS WE AGREED WERE NOT THERE)

It is a concept tossed around in legal circles that "the risk perceived is the duty defined." Meaning generally that the duty or obligation for a party to act is fashioned upon or a function of the foreseeable risk. And of course, now that I have said that I will get letters, emails and a social media torrent from my attorney friends informing me that I got it all wrong somehow. I love the law! It makes me laugh sometimes, other times it makes me cry. I am kidding here, mostly, as the legal system we have in the United States is simply second to no other and I hold its officers of the court in the highest regard. This particular concept though is I think a very interesting one, for if cast too broadly in our casual discourse could become a chronic condition if it hasn't already started well on its way to becoming one.

We often hear that "perception is reality," and I realize the point one tries to make with the phrase. However, some of us it seems take this quite literally and indeed some of the more unscrupulous among us use this fallacy to construct the architecture of their misdeeds. For clarity's sake, we all know that strictly speaking, perception is how we envision and process reality and it can be an accurate depiction of reality, or an inaccurate one. Again, that inaccuracy can be used to mislead on occasion and if that becomes a pattern of behavior, well then we are in the realm of snake oil salesmen. Worse still, if this behavior infuses itself as even moderately accepted thinking in our culture generally, like say reality TV, then we are really in trouble. That's where "The Risk Perceived" was born.

I think it's best we all not become too cozy with little "fibs" or white lies of commission or even omission for, as they say, the worst lies are told in silence. If we get too used to accepting altered facts we are bound to come up with some very unsavory decisions and outcomes. So in "The Risk Perceived", I suggest that before we poison the scales of our thinking in society generally, we consider how we might feel if it were a matter of our own deepest concerns that hung in the balance, and exactly how finely calibrated we would want that device to be. Bending the facts and stretching the truth are all little lubricated code words for placing invisible weights against the fulcrum. And altering our language for political correctness further exasperates the problem of establishing the real truth through these intellectual weights and measures.

THE RISK PERCEIVED (THE THINGS WE AGREED WERE NOT THERE)

They say, "The risk perceived is the duty defined"
Ah what prejudicial slight of hand is perception!
What of that not perceived, or those left behind?
Voiceless prisoners to this tyrannical transgression.

To what or to whom do we collectively owe
Those victims of lies of omission?
An excuse perhaps fit for a serpents tongue
Just nod, wink and hiss your complicit permission.

What lives shall we imprison with this dearth of clear vision?
Or can the unknown truly do us no harm?
A moral compass is a must that perhaps we might trust
Finely calibrated to sound the alarm.

But who could truly resist to give fate's hands a twist?
While prudent concerns remain far more confined.
Questioning who's next to be burned, should the tables be turned,
When my life is yours and your life is mine!

For if "the risk perceived is the duty defined"
It serves us best to be keenly aware
That the risk we all run, when it's all said and done
Where The Things we Agreed Were not There.

As I Am

One morning I was online scanning the news and social media for what was going on both within and beyond the headlines. If you do this from time to time you will find that we are all directed, in not so subtle ways, to take sides on things. Anything and everything and there are polls taken for just about every topic under the sun and we are asked to take a side and stake our claim. This gets a bit mind-numbing after not too long a while, as if we honestly needed yet another way to divide ourselves as a people. Some of the division, especially in social media, can be downright vile and dangerous. So I thought it might be good to arm ourselves with a very short and to-the-point piece to fire back at those judgmental types who apparently sit up in their unchallenged unexamined lair and breathe their rarified air while highlighting for us all of our flaws in splendidly over-magnified fashion. It might be good for those geniuses to remember that someone with capacities far beyond their depth created that which they are so openly critical of and hold in such scorn.

AS I AM

...Well then, you should write my maker,
If your feelings are that strong.
Tell Him just how you'd make me so much better,
Tell Him all the things that He got wrong.

For I'm sure He'd like to hear from you
One so beyond the reach of shame.
So be true to who you send it to,
And be sure to sign your name...

Yes, you know who you will send it to,
And please mention me by name.

CROSSROADS

In "Crossroads" I deal with a concept of the theoretical sciences that postulates that alternative realities could exist, at once, on alternative timelines with each reality in each timeline being as real and viable as the others. These alternative timelines play out in linear time, day by day, on the same days and at the same exact point in universal time. Under these theories the same person, the same Chris for example, would be living out the very same days as the alternative Chris or Chris' at the very same time along different concurrent timelines. Also, in all of these concurrently unfolding timelines all the variables of competing decisions and actions are played out. So, in one timeline our Chris chooses a soda, and in the other lemonade. In one timeline our Chris is a businessman and in another a singer/songwriter and so on. All these combinations and possible permutations are played out and exist simultaneously along separate and distinct timelines which never intersect.

However, in "Crossroads," I consider what might happen if two of these timelines did indeed for some unknown reason intersect, but only long enough for a short, and in this case, interrupted conversation between the two same individuals. In "Crossroads" the two same individuals come upon each other on a street corner on a rainy cold and foggy night near a street-side storefront window. Neither even remotely having in mind any of this "alternative timeline stuff" as they are just going about their day. Indeed, it seems as the two timelines become closer and closer, but before they intersect, one of the characters attempts to reach the other by calling to him, but to no avail—until, of course, the timelines intersect at their "Crossroads."

The conversation that they have on that fateful street corner begins to raise the veil on their unusual situation as their uncanny commonality is very curious to both of them. A commonality so very strong but yet they, in their experience, have only just met, and yet, they feel an immediate and dire need for the other and his well-being; a need that cannot be fulfilled.

During the conversation, it becomes apparent that the decisions made by one of the characters has led him to a much better place in life than the other, and he is disturbed at the sense that he is intimately connected to his new found friend to whom time has not be so equally kind. So what started as a conversation perceived by two strangers to be in the normal course, turns out to be a disturbing and unresolved mystery to both. Also, to further the complexity of the event, because alternative timelines are never supposed to meet, there exists the very real possibility that the entire conversation they thought they had did not really happen at all, or if it did for that brief conversation, it was immediately washed away at the speed of light; in this case the light of a passing car at the "Crossroads," leaving a single lonely soul with a disturbing unresolved feeling while out on a walk on a dreary and misty rain-soaked night.

CROSSROADS

I saw a familiar face on my walk last night, like an echo that had long since faded away. It was a curious embrace as our minds began to chase, history's minions that brought us to this place. Fate was the author of our crossing, and the purveyor of an unrelenting task. Like the mystery and wonder, of a baby fallen under, the yearning to know yet knowing not what to ask.

And frozen in this time and space,
The awkward search for words of grace,
Betrayed the truth revealed by our own eyes.

And as time released her sands again,
The unwinding of the story began,
And released unwitting prisoners from their desperate disguise.

I said, " I'd like to say time has been your friend,
And that your smile seems to have no end,
But I sense that this is not exactly so.

Once forgotten and forsaken,
Your spirit has been shaken,
Please don't ask me just how I've come to know."

He said, "I've watched you walk by here before,
Every night missing you more and more,
But you just would not lend to me your eyes.

I have walked a thousand miles with you;
I've tasted your tears and your love so true,
And found myself in your laughter and your sighs."

I said, "How could it be I've not seen you here,
And have I grown blind to one so near?
You see I feel like I have known you all my life!

In your face I see the years gone by,
And a path that would cast our lives aside,
So we sank into this place of pain and strife.

Are you a person that I could have been?
Are there lessons I need to learn again?
And please tell me that there may still be some time!

For I fear I cannot lose you,
And believe me when I say it's true,
To walk from here alone I can't abide."

I said, "Let us stay together,
We will be so close forever,
Just think of how together we could grow!"

But light conspired with time again,
To wash my reflected life-long friend,
From the storefront window that he used to know...

For while our lives take one direction,
What is hidden from detection,
Is revealed by a reflection when we find,

That there are lives that we're not meant to see,
With infinite possibilities,
On this Crossroads of another place in time.

In Baltimore and Beyond

I speak quite a bit in this book on the topic of self-worth and the importance of the effort of seeking out the better parts of ourselves as people. This kind of message can often times be summarily cast off as candy coated rubbish and unrealistic blatherings. But I humbly submit that if we spent more time and effort, especially in the mass media, installing and supporting the power each of us has as a vehicle for change, we could begin to confront the tyrant of hopelessness right in our own backyards before it has a chance to poison the minds of our energetic youth. This empowerment would also go a long way to inoculating our young minds and hearts from the contrived shouts of the imported hate baiters who are paid to show up where there is trouble, and stoke the fires of division. These hate-baiters couldn't care less about the community, its people or its future. They are as an infection is to an injury; we should be wary of their insidious effects and reveal them for what they are at the earliest sign of their arrival.

I grew up in the suburbs of Maryland and graduated with my degree in business from The University of Baltimore. I look back on my time there with joy and appreciation for all the value the experience and education it brought to my life. Baltimore, Maryland is indeed a charming city and the people who live there are proud and hardworking souls. I have no doubt that the spirit of Baltimore will rise up and successfully defeat the masters of division that currently dwell within and without.

In Baltimore and Beyond

If its a voice you seek,
then learn to use it.

If its love that you need,
learn to give it.

And do not throw the brick,
but work to lay it.

Do not shatter the window,
learn to frame it.

For, if its Peace that you seek,
then learn to seek it in peace,
and you will find it when you have created it.

If its light that you want,
then shine it in truth,
on the fears and the fires that betrayed it.

When your capacity to give exceeds your willingness to take
When your ability to create exceeds your willingness to destroy
When your Spirit seeks the light and rejects the tyranny of heat
And when your actions are guided by good conscience
Then you will have found the way through the frustration,
beyond the flames of buildings and the ruins of dreams,
to the New City, and the new future we can all build together,
"In Baltimore and Beyond!"

What Splendid Prisons We Make

It's been my experience that far too often we are the architects of the very obstacles that hold us trapped from accomplishing some of the most meaningful things we would like to do. We do this as a natural defensive mechanism that is born out of the trials and tribulations of life, the frustrating outcomes we label as failures or the insults or harsh words that stung and left a mark upon our psyche. We become a bit face-shy which can be healthy but usually only in small doses. If we become too defensively protective and conservative, the walls thicken; the windows once open to the world of change and growth close in and our experience grows smaller and darker and of course more frustrating. This is the prison that we can make for ourselves if we allow it. It feels like a safe fortress at first, but after a short time, we explorers at heart, begin to miss the wind-swept taste of fresh opportunities.

So, rather than build stronger fortresses that morph into prisons and dungeons of the down-hearted, let's eliminate the hurt we dispense upon one another that gave rise to the idea of needing such thickly propped up protective walls in the first place. To the extent we act with respect for each other to the best extent we can, giving room for all of us to have bad days now and then, we can eliminate much of the unnecessary friction that slows our pace to a path that reveals many of the same fruits we all desire. In this way, not getting in each other's way is to understand that teamwork is required as well as ones individual responsibility within and to that team. The game is ours to lose or win, and we can win it if we stick together. When we get in each other's way we give up easy points to anyone or anything that would see us fail. Again, the choice, the answer, the solution lies within us.

WHAT SPLENDID PRISONS WE MAKE

Consider for a moment what Splendid Prisons We Make:

We build them strong and sturdy,
To protect our hearts from another emotional violation,
Something else to endure,
Another injury to heal,
Another way to think,
Another question to trouble the night,
As a burdened head befalls a cool welcoming pillow.

Yet with all of this, we all; all of us are survivors! And even without understanding it completely, we instinctively know the available escape routes from these prisons we make, for we are the designers and the architects of their structure. They are our nemesis.

If there is going to be a jail break, if we seek a flight towards freedom, it means tearing down the walls between the you's and the me's, no matter what it shall take! Let us embrace one another and if only for our children's sake.
Let us throw off the shackles and dry up the tears
And lay low the walls that surround
These Splendid Prisons We Make.

A Place for All of These Things

"Everything has its place." If you could see my desk right now as I frantically type away at this book you might think, "Really, Chris, all evidence to the contrary." I admit right now writing to you my mind is as engaged and flowing as my desk is in a state that could best be described as "semi-disheveled eclectic freestyle controlled chaos with a purpose." Ok, actually it looks like a sonic boom went off in here but let's not fixate. It is comforting to know that time is there so we don't have to do everything at once. It's equally comforting that space is there so that we don't have to do it all in the same place. It's with those very simple ideas that I think it's a good idea to savor the things we assign ourselves to; savor the moment and let yourself live in it as opposed to living in its memory when gazing back at it through the time machine of photo images (we used to use the word *photographs* but since I've recently become so hip and with it, *photo images* it is!). We do everything too fast these days and I know it's all been said a million times before, but trust me, slow it down and drink it in before you begin to see the bottom of the glass. I do. I really do. When my time comes and the bottom of the glass is in my view, I want to welcome it as a place to rest after passionately and hungrily tugging at every thread of vibrant energy of this existence I can. I suppose I can be exhausting in this way sometimes but what the heck, let's you and me take this life, this wonderful life, yours and mine out for a walk. If the moment is a quiet relaxing one, melt into it. If it calls you out and taps every mental discipline you have, focus like a laser on it. If you are in competition for something, say a job for instance, bring every cell of yourself into the arena and get after it, all the while knowing that win or lose, that "competition itself is the stone upon which we all may sharpen our skills, the fire in which we can temper our constitution and the gauge with which we can measure our growth." (that's a Chrisism by the way, one of which I am quite proud and since I've had the opportunity to write a book, I just hadda get it in there.) While you're at it, be grateful that the living world all around you does this as well. The butterfly waits for its moment, the bird in the nest awaits its first walk on the wind, the moon is infinitely patient keeping its vigil for the romantic, the sheer mountain sides await your voice to call out your echo; "Carpe diem," seize the day to be sure, but savor the moment my dear friends and enjoy your place to be and a place for all of these things.

A Place for All of These Things

There's a place in the night for all lovers.
There's a place on each face, for the trail of a tear.
There's a place for joy and laughter;
A place for courage and a place for fear.

There's a place where we all stumble,
And a place where we might fall.
A place of unbridled conviction;
And a place to wonder why we try at all.

Yet there are shores where rising waters,
Make love to thirsty sands,
And high swept winds to carry the clouds,
To some other distant lands.

There are waters that frolic with laughter,
Where it's playtime under the sky.
It's a place to hear the voice and the song
Of the dolphin's lullaby.

There's a place for the Earth to tumble,
Through time on invisible wings.
Where eternity is home to the humble,
And A Place for All of These Things.

TENACITY

Webster defines the word tenacious as "holding together firmly" and "clinging to" and also as "retaining." I define it as "it's 12:30 a.m. and I typing away on my book, dare I say tenaciously?" Winston "Never Give In" Churchill of course was a fan of this word and indeed so many wonderful things have been created by the tenacious types. The kind of person that understands what other's refer to as failed attempts actually represent one more step closer to finding the successful approach now that yet another unsuccessful one has been eliminated. It's that mindset that will not allow the poisonous nature of the word failure to creep in to a process. For failure to come into play the struggle must be over; therefore, if you never surrender your will to proceed yet again and again, failure will be forced to keeps its distance. Failure cannot exist when the tenacious are at the top of their game.

I've said, somewhere in this book, I forget where, but please promise me you'll keep looking for it, tenaciously, that "patience can only find her rest when her silent vigil has found its reward." So you can see that in my opinion, patience and tenacity are intrinsically related in application. I bring this up because in writing "Tenacity" I was thinking of how impatient we are quickly becoming. I think the downward spiral started with freeze-dried instant coffee, but I could be wrong. We are getting so accustomed to everything being more and more "instant" that our ability to see things through to their conclusion patiently is experiencing atrophy, just wilting away due to lack of use. It comes as no surprise that researchers now tell us in studying the effects of social media online, for example, that spending time online acts like an addictive drug; if you check your online social whatever and there is no message then the gland in your brain responsible for your mood adjusts your mood downward, but if you just got a direct message your mood swings up. At least until you get the message that nobody likes your last post and then you get depressed again. So we are allowing our yearning for immediate gratification or results of some kind to erode away that wonderful shield against failure we call tenacity.

Social media is just one of the culprits in the corrosion of tenacity. The list goes on and probably comes as an extension of our efforts to handover the mundane yet necessary tasks of living to machines so we can go about the elegant and advanced things like advancing medicine, creating art and architecture, exploring space. So while the things that can erode our tenacious spirit may have come from otherwise noble efforts we must be careful not to let them begin to dictate our capacity of strenuous and arduous effort whose fruits are not immediately manifest.

So in writing "Tenacity" I wanted to sing the praises of the tenacious types but also remind people that before you give up on some task consider that you may not realize that the next little bit of effort may be all it takes to put you over the goal line. It seems such a simple concept but Ockham teaches us that often the simplest among competing solutions is usually the one to go with, and history tells us it is often the most powerful. So stay in the game and hold your course.

"When the keel is deep, the course is true and the ship is strong,

Fill your sails with the wildest wind, challenge the sea, and Sail On."
- *Sail On*, by Chris Mentch

Tenacity

For all that can be taken,
Or surrendered under force.
Unless otherwise they are forsaken,
Shall return in all due course.

For when the battle is exhausted,
It may well be a sin.
That while next in line to victory,
The victor just gave in.

For victory is the constant,
Of the tenacious soul.
That understands divinities hands,
And sees failure too great a toll.

It is the dreamer that shapes the future,
As the sculptor shapes the clay.
To create the art of an inspired heart,
And a vision of a better way.

THE NIGHT OF THE MAGICAL CHRISTMAS HARE

I am a romantic sap. No, that's wrong. I am a hopelessly romantic sap. That's step one right? The first step in addressing a problem is admitting you have one. It's not really so much a problem though if you don't mind getting your heart strings tugged at more than a few times in a day. Actually, it's a condition with which I have always been quite comfortable. Romantic in the more classical and direct sense of the word of course. Allowing oneself to be comfortable in matters of the heart with another is a very good measure of self-assured compassionate strength and refined character in my humble opinion and I try to play the role of the "Mensch" at all times; shameless pun fully intended. It's a great way to be! But what I am really getting at is that use of the term that indicates an openness to the imaginary or visionary; a more free-wheeling and less restricted approach to seeing things. Allowing some things to take the fashion and form in their most expressive.

Most of us with this condition or blessing, you make the call, get a bit intoxicated in the richness of culture and history, ceremony and solemn meaning of Christmas. The Earth takes on a form unlike anything we are used to during the year. The sunlight falls at what seems to be a more introspective angle at the earth and casts all things in a new light and all creatures to a new sense of being and belonging. Told ya I was a sap.

"The Night of the Magical Christmas Hare" also shows my absolute love of animals and in this case, bunnies. I've owned many rescues in my time . . . strike that, many bunnies have adopted and trained me

83

in my time, just as any dog lover or cat lover worth their salt has come to find in their training. So bunny lover that I am, I simply took the liberty to place them in a poem to the cadence of *T'was the Night Before Christmas* and let my romantic sap imagination fly. Intellectually I just let go and I let the emotion of the story as it might unfold just flow from my pen. Honestly, but for one verse that I needed to "glue" the activity of the Mighty Bunny walking around the Flying Christmas Quilt it is a one draft poem.

By the time my hand hit its scribbling stride at the beginning of the second verse it took the story down a path that placed a little embedded mystery within the timeline. As anyone who has ever been in a heavy snowfall, especially a peaceful and heavy snow with little or no wind, the world around you gets very quiet being wrapped in the insulation of the snow. At this point in the poem, just before the bunnies are startled by the rustling, "time seems to move ever slower and slower." This line sets up the possibility that the rest of the poem, indeed the whole visit, was merely a bunny dream that began with this magical and whimsical Christmas Bunny, Geese and Quilt.

I mention the idea that the spirit of Christmas, of Peace on Earth, should live on throughout the year with mention of the Easter Bunny and close the story by reinforcing that securing that peace is something we must all do and we should do it for one another. I will admit, in all seriousness something about this piece, as I wrote it brought me to tears. I am a romantic sap but not generally a weeping one.

The Night of the Magical Christmas Hare

T'was the night before Christmas and all through the warren,
Not a bunny was stirring Grandpa Rabbit lie snorin'.
The juniors all snuggled together in their nests,
And labored to stay still at their mothers' behest.
The stockings swayed from branches of the tree by their lair,
Awaiting the arrival of the Magical Christmas Hare.

The shadows fell softly as the night wrapped around,
A peaceful stillness settled in and the bunnies bedded down.
A heavy snow was now falling and the bows now hung lower,
It seemed time began to move ever slower and slower.
The air then fell silent in the cold winters chill,
And the earth kept her vigil, as time then stood still.

When a rustling broke the still and the quiet of night,
From overhead it befell us so it caused quite a fright!
Then came a light thumping we could barely hear,
So we listened much tighter, we perked up our ears!
On this white night of wonder bathed in light soft as fleece,
Our eyes fell upon the Magical Christmas Bunny and his nine white
snow geese!

These geese seemed to shimmer in the new fallen snow,
Their eyes seemed to twinkle; their down seemed to glow.
What a message from heaven they and this hare must bring,
Like the stardust that sparkles upon their great wings.
As he tended his winged team with hugs and with treats,
We marveled at the size of this bunnies feet!

And much more magical than any sleigh ever built,
The geese pulled this bunny on a flying Christmas quilt!
Each square carefully sewn but not quite by hand,
But by paw, hoof and feathered wings from all over the land.
Bound together with magic to dazzle the eyes,
And help messengers of the Christmas Spirit to fly!

He returned to his quilt and then hopped to the back,
And pulled with great might at an over-flowing sack.
It was filled with toys musical that made Christmas bells ring,
Fit for Knights Queens and Lords and the mightiest of Kings.
I spied one gift I thought was surely a rose,
A closer look revealed a toy reindeer with a big shining nose!

He filled up our stockings each and every one,
With treats and toys with frolic and fun.
Then suddenly he turned and to our surprise,
He began to speak and with a twinkle in his eyes, he said:
"The Spirit of Christmas lives for animals too!"
And with his ears he pointed, "it's for you, you and you!"

"It's for eagles and whales, from snails to my geese,
In the brotherhood of creatures we must all live in peace!"
Since bunnies spend so much time running in fear,
These wise words of kindness were so good to hear.
"We are all a great family and each plays a part,
Bringing meaning to our lives and warmth to our hearts."

He said; "This message is important so lend me your ears,
You must help it live on throughout the year."
"When the days turn from cold to warmer and sunny,
As a reminder I will send my friend Easter Bunny."
Let the spirit of ALL seasons be "peace on earth,
As flowers bloom in the spring with the meadows rebirth."

Then he returned to his magical quilted night-flyer,
The geese spread their wings and flew higher and higher.
His voice echoed through the stars as they twinkled in the night.
"Merry Christmas to all and to all a Good Life!"
We sat in stunned silence, we wanted so him to stay,
But knew he would return in a year to the day.

Legend says when the snow falls so heavy that the passes are filled,
He comes to visit the silent little souls that live in the hills.
And in this setting pure and white as a dove,
He fills us all with warmth by the glow of his love.
So whether it's delivered by geese or reindeer,
The meaning of the season is alive and clear...

It's a message from the heavens, it's the dust from the stars.
It's a mission of Peace on Earth that is ours.

The Mentch rescue bunnies Co Co, Checkers, Madison and Checkmate
Original drawing of the Mentch family bunnies by Courtney Murphy

LEGACY

So often, and especially in the realm of Presidential politics, we will hear of someone concerned about their legacy and what exactly will be their crowning achievement? It often seems to me to be a little bit late to be considered seriously as the question most often arises near the end of some politician's final term in office. Not limited to politics of course, we often wind up *confronting the spectre* of our legacy too late in the game as opposed to *embracing the opportunity* to construct that legacy in the early years. I thought, when writing my piece "Legacy," what exactly would be a great concept to be understood deeply by a newborn just entering this world and what wonderful prospects they might have if they knew what potential they embodied and the time they had to maximize it? Perhaps in that way a person could truly feel empowered and be less afraid or timid or even more importantly less malleable to by those who come to them in this life with nefarious intent.

A legacy is an achievement constructed over a lifetime and every day of that life is another valuable brick to be laid in that life's construction. It is therefore a powerful reminder of how valuable each day is in the tapestry of our lives more broadly and not just something to be worried about in a panic when time is running out. So if you haven't already started, then start writing your legacy today!

LEGACY

You come from all that has ever been.
You are part of all that there is, and how it shall be.
Your life, your story, will be part of all that ever was.
A unique spark, in every light that has ever shined.
What shall you choose to do with this gift?

May your eyes forever see beyond the limits of light's ambition.
May your wings carry you to the farthest reach of your imagination
and dreams.
May your heart forever be the welcoming temple of limitless compassion.
And may the Spirit of love and of life, always bring you peacefully back home.

The time is now, to write your story.
The day has come to reach for your dream.
The Temple Body, is the vessel given,
To embrace love, as a way of living.

And with this, claim now, your Legacy.

LOVE ONE ANOTHER EVEN MORE

In "Love One Another Even More," the reader or listener will immediately come to know that yours truly is all in with astronomy and space exploration/science. They are visually and philosophically beautiful studies interwoven with the emotional element of answering questions that have eluded mankind for so very long. They challenge the intellect on a scale unimaginable and require us to open ourselves and our thoughts well past those of our day to day understanding of things. In pursuing their study all things we know are cast in a whole new light with completely revised context. We are finding our place in it all and perhaps answering the age old question of "why are we here?" It is an outward exploration of the unknown to learn more about our inner-selves and therefore, ultimately, an introspective exercise. Peering outward toward beauty and mystery to better understand who we are as individuals, what is our place in it all, and why do we care so very much about someone or something, we know not what exactly, that may or may not exist outside of ourselves. Why do we have the sense that we are part of something larger than ourselves; and why does this sound and feel so very much like falling in love?

Our senses strain to give us hints of this when we first meet someone and yet we have this overwhelming feeling that we have met them before or that they have somehow been in our lives all the while playing some role and only now have come to our realization. I believe that this experience of seeking outward while not knowing exactly what we are seeking is the subconscious quest to complete what we intuitively know; that we as individuals are not yet complete. We are aware of a void in our sense of being that can only be filled by something or someone outside of ourselves. Put another way, to become complete

90

we must give ourselves over to and allow ourselves to accept another. We intuitively realize that our existence is part of a lovely grand design, and in the completion of that design we seek our part, our reason, and extend our spiritual and emotional selves toward the beauty and life of another. We have begun the process of becoming one with something and someone outside of our own person. It is far beyond being fruitful and multiplying. It is in my mind a quest for home. We have extended our concern and our reason for being into *loving another even more*, than we love ourselves.

In the "whispered shimmering radiance" where we come to understand the relationships of things so beyond our immediate physical experience; where time and space are elements of the fabric upon which we live, so too we come to understand the eternal quest of the soul that must, to complete itself, find its home in the heart of another.

LOVE ONE ANOTHER EVEN MORE

I've known you longer than my memory allows
I've loved you stronger than my inner strength somehow
I've been with you in places deeper than the darkest sea
But how can you be closer, than I am to me?

There are places darkly shining through the firmament of space
Whispered shimmering radiance needing neither time nor place
Hailing beyond the reach or measure of times falling sands
The spirited breath of life itself splashed upon these loving hands

Where the yearning and the passion that can traverse the great expanse
Completes the timeless mystery of love and luck and chance
A beacon of light eternal, guiding solemn leaps of faith
To the challis overflowing, perfected "glory is but grace..."

The life that lives within us is hard to understand
Its origin and destiny take us to uncharted lands
And it is there where we gather upon some far and distant shore
Where we care for ourselves deeply, yes, but,
Love One Another Even More!

ANGELS OF MERCY

"Blessed are the peacemakers." Indeed. Let it be so!

On a fateful September day, the lives of thousands of American innocents were taken from us. It was appropriate I suppose that the day was so very clear as that which played out before our very eyes deserves all the clarity and focus that history can record, lest we ever forget. For on that day evil visited the sun-kissed shores of our homeland, well within the shining and welcoming beacon on Lady Liberty's torch. So stark was the contrast of good and evil in the bright white light of that crystal morning. Once again, American exceptionalism like the sun would shine, proving again to a watchful world that America is still, and forever will be, the best and greatest hope for the peaceful future of this lovely planet and its people. Let it be so!

History is now replete with examples of how America triumphs over the dark forces that confront her. As the pages turn and the next chapters are written, America proves, again and again, how the toughest challenges of her age bring out the very best in her proud people so diverse in their cultures and heritage. Let it be so!

May God forever hold the souls of those taken too soon from us on that day in his eternal loving care.

May we always remember the bravery, selflessness and sacrifice of all the first responders.

And may our Lord forever bless The United States of America!

93

Let it be so.

This piece is dedicated to the firefighters, law enforcement personnel, and others who faced the unspeakable horror of terrorism with immeasurable courage and compassion.

ANGELS OF MERCY

There is no greater level of courage, no deeper measure of compassion, than that shown by those who rush willingly headlong into harm's way to illuminate the darkness brought on by evil's black fire with the pure white light of their brightest angels. It is to these brave souls that America stands forever indebted. Their actions have strengthened our resolve to answer the challenges of aggression and terror and defeat them at every turn. They have deepened our commitment to our country and our compassion to our fellow countrymen. They have done no less than to lift a nation swollen with pride to greater heights with the ever-rising wind swell of freedom. Our hearts are at once heavy with the great weight of loss, yet our collective spirits rise easily upon the wings of these gallant Angels of Mercy.

SHIPS IN BOTTLES

In "Ships in Bottles" I deal with the truly meaningful roles we can play among the many that compete for our time and energy and passion. Some of these, while intoxicating to the senses in their perceived grandeur or immediate impact in the consensus view and style of the time, are set in their proper context as our lives unfold by events and actions that transcend what is, at the time, considered in high-fashion and allure. I also deal with the frustration that while our lives unfold we often grapple with the reality that for whatever reason unknown to us as individuals, we are in some instances unable to do all the things we were clearly, by design, meant to do, or we are unable or withheld from experiencing the events we were meant to experience to play our intended role with the talents and gifts we were originally given. This latter point can be and has been interpreted by some who have read this poem to apply to our special needs brothers and sisters, but need not be limited to only those instances; for indeed many special needs persons in our history have played the heroic roles once they have been granted just a little compassion. Indeed, they more frequently than not, teach us the true limitless and tenacious nature of the human spirit and return a gift to us all for which we will strive a lifetime in which to be worthy.

I also point out in the piece, the importance of seemingly random acts of kindness that in so many cases release a suffering person from the yoke of their burden with an act that is powerful and indeed elegant and eloquent in its clarity of purpose and simplicity of its delivery. The power to grant the freedom to another among us to be the person that they were meant to be and the person that they strive to be is held by the "Child King of One Kind Deed," and that Child King my friends can be you and it can be me.

So while there are ships of great wealth and ships of great conflicts at sea that build industry and shape nations, it can be seen that the these pursuits while notable in their time in the immediate and while important are still, by comparison trivial, to the ship, that has just this minute found its ultimate treasure, its entire future and its true purpose; that being of course, its freedom to sail.

SHIPS IN BOTTLES

It's a mystery to all seafarers,
of just how she got inside.
But now this ship within a bottle,
must find a safe place to hide.

She rocks and rolls upon waters,
she cannot touch, nor can she abide.
She is at home alone, where no waves will flow;
No moon and no ebb tide.

Like a fish left out of water;
Like a bird without the air.
She now begins to wonder,
just how did she get there?

Was it a cruel quirk of nature,
that put her in this place?
With winds her sails cannot feel,
and ocean spray she cannot taste.

No course correction, nor need for reflection,
for this wayward vessel to sail.
For the conditions are never changing,
within her crystal jail.

No new horizons or even green water,
to wash across her bow.
No stars at night, just this endless fight,
She asks, "How much will this bottle allow?"

Then pulled from the sand, by a small child's hand,
she's a treasure for a young boy to see.
As he shatters the bottle with his special stone,
and sets his new friend free.

Now there are tales of avarice and conquest;
Of great victories at war.
And the ships that sail through struggle and strife,
building wealth that nations will store.

But they are worthless trivialities,
for the Child King of One Kind Deed.
You see these are the dreams of all those Ships
In bottles with Special Needs.

In the Face of Her Storm

Written in the abstract, "In the Face of Her Storm" is a short piece about love and faith growing stronger through the tumult of struggle and challenge. The "tender ship" mentioned in the poem represents someone giving care and comfort to another during the fury of the struggle both are facing together. Tender ships, of course, are ships whose purpose is to "tend" to the needs of other ships of other specialties. Tender ships provide supplies and repairs and other services to ships at sea so that those other vessels functions and operations can be repaired or attended to for whatever reason, without undue danger to vessels at sea or delay or impairment of the scheduled ship's course.

So often people, whether just friends or in love relationships or for that matter complete strangers with no close relation of any kind, find that going through very challenging times in life together creates a special bond; indeed playing the role of the "tender person" in someone's life can be a truly enriching experience. There is really nothing quite like facing challenges with someone especially if what they are facing is serious or grave and perhaps would otherwise overwhelm them if the "tender person" were not there. It's those stories we read about when someone of rather meek physical build can hoist a tractor from the underpinned victim after a tornado levels smalltown USA. These instances allow a person to step well beyond their physical, and actually more often is the case, their emotional limits to come to the immediate aid of someone for which they care deeply.

The piece is a short and straightforward poem for sure, but that's a nice change now and then and I thought it proper as the personality types of the rescuers for which I write are, almost to a person, the humble "ah shucks" type, that really know how to pour on the care and courage when the real chips are down. The kind of character that is strong enough to deliver the tender touch during a raging maelstrom. What would we do without them?

In the Face of Her Storm

Maroon flags are flyin'.
The wind is not our friend.
And SOS is the only message,
That this tender ship will send.

The waves are high and rugged,
Taking green water over the bow.
Can we survive this demons pounding?
If so I don't know how!

I struggled down through the galley.
And again up to the mast.
I even checked on the dunsel,
Wrapped my girl's sails down, I wrapped 'em low and I wrapped 'em fast.

I've rocked in this sea's loving arms,
But I've also felt her scorn.
I am humbled, yes, but my faith grows stronger,
Here, In the Face of Her Storm.

JUST ANOTHER DAY

Oh how we take our days too often for granted. "How was your day?" "Oh, just another day, you know." We all do it and I am perhaps as guilty as anyone. I try not to fall into that habit though. I study economics now and then and its concepts and axioms are actually quite useful in day to day living. For example when items are abundant price generally falls. Put another way the value we assign to plentiful things tends to be lesser than had those same things been in short supply. Heaven forbid that some illness or accident limits the time we have, but when it does we suddenly awaken to the value of the day. Indeed, I stand in humbled awe at those courageous people who become ill and espouse a new and enlightening outlook in that they say that they have never really "lived" like they do now that their days are limited; every moment, in their far more clear view, a treasure. We should all listen and hold closely their wisdom and seriously consider the promise and opportunity each blessed day offers. If you've gotten this far in this book you are no doubt hoping with all your hoping might that I don't go on for twelve pages on that point, so mercifully, I will restrain myself. It's enough to say that the beauty and elegance of the gift of a day, rain or shine, should be cherished whether we have but one day left or years and years to be together. So I thought that maybe, just maybe, this poem might be a good thing to flashback upon when we all fall into that trap of taking for granted the gift we have been given. Let me also offer up this idea. Try to write your own "Just Another Day" poem and allow yourself the chance to actually put on paper what your day means to you.

JUST ANOTHER DAY

Throw me through the stars
Roll me in your dreams
This universe is ours
Bathed in cosmic flowing streams

Catch me if you can
On the other side tonight
Hold on lightly to my hand
Like shadows cling to the quickening light

Frost upon a flower
Laughter's tears melt in the sun
And as hour chases hour
Her chariot's stallions have begun

To seek the cradle of forever
Asking questions never posed
In rooms where walls are but illusions
Whose phantom doors shall never close

Upon silvered wings of splendor
We fly this dream on through the night
Quenching our thirst and hungry yearning
Beneath drenching waves of sweet delight

GALILEO, GALILEE

Galileo is considered the father of modern observational astronomy and he lived in an era of scientific advancement and study that challenged the way the world and the powers that existed at the time saw things and at times allowed others to see things. He died at the age of 77 in 1642. His theories of heliocentrism; or the idea that the sun, as opposed to the earth, resides at the center of our solar system was not accepted by many in his time. To say that he was challenged in his beliefs is an enormous understatement. His list of accomplishments and contributions to helping us understand our world includes discovering and mapping the orbits of Jupiter's four closest moons, appropriately enough called the Galilean satellites; the phases of Venus; the analysis of sunspots; he was a student of music, mathematics and in my thinking, of the very rhythm of life and the waltz of the stars through eternity. And while so much of his accomplishments were actual visual observations as were the limits of the technology of his time, he later in his life lost a good share of his vision which just seems so unfair considering how well he put it to use. He saw so very much, he shared so very much, often courageously and with the style of the passionate Italian that he was.

Around the time I wrote "Galileo, Galilee" I was reading about the great scientific explorers of the past and at the same time reading The Bible and the miracles that Jesus performed on the shores of the Sea of Galilee. The over-arching theme in my mind while reading both was the idea of stretching the human experience and advancement through study, and faith, through hardship and unbridled passion to know and to embrace the beauty and glory of all the wonder around us; the absolute need for equal measures of courage and compassion and to run risks for the betterment of all and to give oneself to the pursuit of truth, and light and love. To see that which does not meet the eye; to understand that which requires faith; to value deeply of the arduous effort to try and to run risks, despite the possibility that while the goal sought may be within reach it may yet still escape our grasp; such amazing people were they!

I place Galileo in the finest of company near the Shores of Galilee in the title of the piece, but these are the people that show us that we are not slaves to the tyrant of ignorance or to the prince of darkness. They teach us that our passion for learning and exploring, our capacity for faith and mercy, and indeed our intrinsic connection to each other and to the vast humming universe we all call home, is the hallmark of the human spirit that can both touch deeply the human heart while yet boldly and with humbled and respectful awe, reach outward from this earthly shore, through a sea of stars. In this way we grow, we understand and we find each other, children of the universe in the family of man.

GALILEO, GALILEE

Starlight, star bright,
You think you will,
And I think you might.
Whisper to "Vincent" and McLean,
Of a "Starry, Starry Night."

For you see as a blind man might see.
Speak of the sky, Galileo Galilei,
Speak of the sea,
Galileo, Galilee.

Here burns the truth that can set souls free;
A fire so bright, it might blind,
The tender eyes that seek its crystalline spheres,
Another scar, another find.

Some souls are enslaved by the tyrant of darkness,
Their groaning echo's in Dante's deepening well.
Why is it to speak of the glorious heavens,
We must so often stare into the precincts of hell?

But you can see as the blind man might see!
So speak of the sky,
Galileo Galilei.
Speak of the sea,
Galileo, Galilee.

WHAT TRUE BEAUTY IS

Ah Beauty. Seems like a simple enough concept really, and mankind has surely been around long enough to figure it out if it isn't. I mean we have figured out the glorious grandeur of the cathedral mountains, the endless expanse of the sky and the living and breathing sea, the towering columns and archways of byzantine delight, but what of you and me?

Well as to us individuals, it seems we are still hard at work on that one. You can indeed spend an entire week in the department store "beauty industry aisle" and never even scratch the surface, something frowned upon in the "beauty industry aisle" (when they frown, which itself is frowned upon), or even hope to mercifully reach the end of the "beauty industry aisle." Yes my friends beauty is *an industry*. And in the marketplace it's a marathon that only the strongest of will and tenacious character can even hope to survive let alone endure. You can pour it on, smear it on, dab it on, rub it in, rub it out, lift it, tuck it, pinch it, dry it up, conceal it, highlight it, moisturize it, groom it, style it, refresh it, swab it, powder it, cream it and do other things I will claim complete and total ignorance of herein.

I am fortunate enough to know many beautiful people. They take care of themselves. They respect themselves. They take care of others. They respect others. They take care of the environment around them. They respect the environment around them. Guys and gals of course, straight and gay, indeed their sexuality doesn't define them anymore than the form of their politics or which goo they buy when they are fortunate enough to escape the "beauty industry aisle," but I digress. Equally of absolutely no distinction is their religious affiliation, their race, their creed; I think you get my point. In fact I have Republican friends and Democrat friends; Protestant, Catholic and Jewish friends; black, white, Latino and Asian friends; straight and gay, liberal and conservative friends. Don't know if I have any Libertarian or Tea Party friends but then again that pesky "Friendship Evaluation Form" hasn't gotten back from the printer just yet. Again, you get my point.

So let me get *to the point*. Here is my description of a few of my beautiful male and female friends. He or she stands for his or her beliefs in the face of the strongest resistance. He or she is one who puts his or herself at great risk to help total strangers, and who neither fears nor is offended by that or those which he or she does not yet fully understand. My beautiful friends are ones whose mere touch gives comfort and whose eyes reveal a thoroughly self-assured soul. My beautiful friends hearts tend to quicken at the thought of his or her deepest held concerns and life's passions, and are those who are open to learning and expanding his or her purview and understanding of this world and each other and are not afraid to risk getting hurt at taking that chance to advance and to grow. My beautiful friends humbly allow that which he or she appreciates in another to be seen and enjoyed in themselves and they grant it openly. My beautiful friends nurture the potential around them and are willing to let the fruits and successes of others grow and celebrate loudly their treasure in the ebb and flow of effort and fulfillment, sacrifice and satisfaction, success and yes failure for even what we call failure is a learning experience when shared. They accept with grace and appreciation the tides bounty and dance in the spray and foam all the while also accepting and expecting that tide to ebb once again. My beautiful friends are willing to shine an honest smile that reflects the energy within and show openly the joy it evokes in others. They know that to be seen and heard, welcomed and understood, that they must be aware and listen, be graciously welcoming and understanding, and to therefore give and receive the best each has to give and to get. My beautiful friends are keenly aware that he or she can most honestly find themselves as reflected in the eyes and in the lives of those they love.

You see, my beautiful friends and I, understand that beauty is a way of being; simple as that. You'd think the "beauty industry aisle" people would have figured it out by now! My dear friends, I have!

What True Beauty Is

A brave soul
A kind heart
An open mind

A tender touch
A confident gaze
The passionate kind

The curious type
A willingness joined
Attraction entwined

The river's release
The flower that opens
And the ocean of sun that they find

The rising waters
The fountains crest
The basin below

Reflecting the smile
On the youthful face
And the beauty he's come to know

The glorious vision before him
It seems the dream was not only his
Only by being and sharing what we are given
Can we then find what true beauty is.

PERSONAL JOURNAL SELECTIONS

Years ago, when I first started putting my original writing "out there," I was prodded to start sharing personal journal entries or to publish them. Of course, the only redeeming value I could think of for such a collection would be the non-medicinal use it could provide in its application to assist insomniacs the world over to fall helplessly into heavy REM sleep dozers. For, while I do lead an examined life, I try to keep the appreciation level high and the drama level on mute. My life is also not a systematically and formally recorded one and if there's a rhythm to my days it is with less than a measured metronomic periodicity and more of a syncopated thing with emphasis added on the back beat.

But since I will try nearly anything at least once, I gave a *monthly journal* a try for a while. I have included them here as a nice way to conclude my first book and my first chat with you all, my new found friends. It seems to flow nicely in that we have covered a fair bit of ground relating to the background and inspiration for my original writing so this goes just a bit farther into simple personal thoughts.

Also, since we have established that yours truly is a romantic sap at heart, I of course love the soulful reflective time of the fall season which is where these entries were taken from a few years ago.

MONTHLY REVIEW KICKOFF

Hello everyone and let me start by saying thank you so much for your wonderful responses to *As I See It!* Your comments have been as generous and complimentary as they have been insightful. I am grateful for your time and the unique perspective each of you bring to the larger conversation. Some of you have been a bit shy about posting to the comments page, but there is no need to be shy here. The comments page is for everyone who would like to join in the discussion, that broad perspective can benefit all who visit. I am gratified to find that *As I See It* has found a home in each of you.

This month, as you know by now, we have announced that we will release my CD in August on iTunes and other entertainment services. The CD is a cross-section of material in that it contains acoustic, electric, unplugged and full band songs. It represents the first musical facet of *As I See It*, and since I wrote all the material, the writing style may seem familiar; however, the content is fresh. I was proud to work with a number of fine musicians and two fantastic studio producers in Mr. Pratt and Mr. Order. We hope you enjoy the collection and you know where to post your feedback.

I'm glad to see that on the poetry side of the site, you enjoyed the range covered by the first full wave of pieces. "Ships in Bottles," for example, seemed to resonate with folks who at some point in their lives where carrying some burden and often not knowing where to turn for help, until some event or person made a difference in their situation or self-perception. Whatever was the catalyst, what they remembered was the person or situation and the feeling of release and joy that in an instant made all things seem new again. I had a stand-out experience of my own a few years ago as well, so in the interest in getting things rolling in our chat let me share that with you now.

I was at a local grocery store here in Southern California, standing in the checkout line of my favorite cashier, Jan. (Doesn't everybody have a favorite cashier?) Ahead of me was an elderly woman who was having her treasures rung up as she fuddled in her purse for her checkbook. This to the chagrin of the folks behind me, glaring back and forth franticly at her, then back again at their watches! There must have been something very exciting goin' on somewhere that I didn't know about because everyone was in a rush, armed with fast track paying plastic of every breed at the ready for warp speed checkout. I noticed that this lady was buying an inordinate amount of beef, steaks, chicken, all sorts of barbeque trimmings as well as candy, cakes and on and on. I thought if it was all for her she would surely explode! I also noticed that despite the large volume of groceries, that there was no husband around or any helper at all. I thought, maybe she's a widow. Perhaps a bit lonely, and throwing a party to get family together. It was then, that no sooner than I got an idea in my head, that cashier Jan through me a look that said she knew I was up to something. She could see the wheels turning in my head as I slowly pulled the divider from between the lady's groceries and mine with the skill and guile of Copperfield. She noticed nothing as she had nearly rescued her checkbook from the very bowels of her handbag. Jan shook her head and smiled and continued to ring things through, the woman's items then mine. Jan knew because I have a bit of a history for such hijinks, and I thought that if I ever do a video for my song "These Fences" I'm putting this scene in! Finally, both her and my items were totaled. By now she had found her checkbook! She looked up at Jan, Jan looked at me, I looked at her and the people behind me looked back at their watches! It was like the scene in an old western just before a shootout. I said, " my name is Chris and if you don't mind I'd like to buy those things for you today." She looked at me, a total stranger as if I had lost my mind. Then her expression warmed to me and the idea. An eternity passed in the next two minutes as I am sure the watches on the folks behind me just stopped. She said, her voice breaking under the weight of a tear that then fell from her eye, "that's the nicest thing anyone has ever done for me." She asked what's my name again and I told her that that wasn't important but what was important was that, "you don't eat all of that at once, just pace yourself, OK?" Her tears yielded to a smile and another of my grocery store favorites, Lauren, finished bagging the woman's things. (Everybody has a favorite grocery store bagger, right?) I went back there a few weeks later and the women had taken the trouble to leave a card for Jan and Lauren to give to me as a thank you. That day, I was the one with the tear in the eye.

I suppose everyday we all have the chance to be the "Child King of One Kind Deed" like the character in Ships in Bottles, with the ability to make all things new again for a stranger with one simple but meaningful act. Kinda makes you feel powerful doesn't it? Well, it should. You are powerful! As long as you have a choice and you keep your brighter angels within reach, you can be the King or Queen for a Day! So choose wisely.

So, let me close out here by thanking you in advance for all the things I'm about to learn from your experiences. All your comments and conversation on the material and how it relates to you or your lives or anything at all that comes to mind as you read or listen is fair game. No judging here. I eagerly look forward to hearing from you all in the new "Your Voices" page, and until then, of course, Peace. Chris

September Journal –
Autumn's Gentle Approach

I love this time of year. I love the way it looks; the way it smells; the way it tastes. It's great to see how people start to rearrange their lives, taking their lead, once again, from mother nature, rearranging the stage our lives play out upon. Nature dresses up the out of doors in a decidedly different and celebratory state of attire. Full vibrant colors for deep contemplation of the richness and treasures she freely grants those of us who are willing to take the time to drink in and to consider. We follow her lead and change our look as well. I'm not an expert on fashion by any means, but even I can see the change in texture, tone and contrast; indeed, I can taste it. From the clothes we wear, to the sleeping grass, to a hillside set in such delightful repose, so beautiful yet so shy she blushes, I can sense it. From the chilled air that transforms words to mist, dew to crystal and whispers to the ponies, "you are all racers! Run ponies run!" It's time for everyone and everything to play "dress-up" and play like the children that we are, but seldom allow ourselves to be. This, my friends, is rebirth.

This time of year things just "look" differently. The sun's angle relative to the earth while always changing is now noticeably different. The shadows are longer; the days shorter. A gentle caring nudge is a great signal to all of us that it is healthy, once in a while, to pause and change our approach or outlook to things around and within us and our relationships to them. How do I effect the lives of those I care about, or people I have just recently met. How have they affected me. "How may I be available to you?" How have I grown? What have I learned? What changes would be good to consider, and of those I've considered, which should I cast aside? To what or to whom will I commit myself to in the coming year and why? What spaces still lay empty in my life and how will I fill them? All this, as a result of autumn's gentle approach.

It's good then, I think, to welcome this gentle season of change with humility and grace. To recognize that we all cast our own shadows by the light of creation, and that that very light still shines deep within each of us. It offers us a chance to simply celebrate "being," and whispers to us all "you are all racers children! Run children, run!!!"

Happy Autumn Everyone, and as always, Peace!
Chris.

October Journal – Transitions, Acceptance and Celebration

First of all let me start by wishing you all a healthy and happy Halloween. A ritual that has its own history that at its core deals with transitions; from one season to another; from one state of mind to another and indeed, from one state of being to another. Marking a connection between life and death and all that symbolizes this contrasting state of being. Indeed, what we now know as Halloween, went through its own transitions and evolutions over time and across cultures and still does so today. It seems, for example, that neighborhood trick or treating door to door is giving way to organized parties where all the ghosts and goblins and hosts of ghosts dwell. It's all good and it's all fun. Personally, I'm more of a Thanksgiving and Christmas kinda guy, but that's for another day. For now, it's a period of transitions, and transitions, more often than not, are accompanied by deep philosophical undercurrents of joy, release and acceptance. This as we all learn one of life's toughest lessons. Just how to hold on, while at the same time, letting go; to mourn while we celebrate; to come together in both the darkness and the light…giving candy, to a ghoul.

Transitions also evoke contrasts. From light to dark but also from warm to cold. From seemingly unending bright yellow summer days that hang in the haze, to their contrasting sisters where long flowing shadows of mystery are more the norm. The summer would have us believe that she goes on forever, however, the approaching chill reminds us in a very healthy way that time is still passing. And that while rest and recreation is a must, that there comes a time to move on again. That time is our friend if we nurture her, but can be onerous if she is left ignored. I strongly reject the notion of some that say "time is a fire in which we all burn." It's more accurate to say that time is a light that the wise ones choose to follow; the essential ingredient to our very humanity and yes, our mortality. Perhaps it is both a strength and a weakness of the human condition. Two opposing sides of the continuum where the fulcrum of living deliberately holds vigil between the two, both securing and preserving a living balance. To guide us with equal measure of joy and restraint; with rapture's yearning and the surrender of satisfaction. In this way our very mortality teaches us of the true gift of life, and this is the crucial point, the gift of life WHILE IT IS OURS TO SHARE. Understanding that as we have fewer hours of light in a day than we have dark, each hour therefor becomes more valuable. The darkness and cold teaches us the urgent value of the NOW, and of TODAY, and that NOW IS FOREVER. Acceptance and transition are intimate friends of growth. Let us all grow together. Happy Halloween!

EPILOGUE

Well here we are and like I said in the preface, I hope we close this book, you and I, more on the level of friends than as we started as reader and author. I truly hope that the fruits of my rather diverse experience in business and music performance writing and entertaining has found a home in your life. I hope that some of what I have observed and learned in my life's experiences and some of what I have opined in this book benefit you in your life and I hope that they do so in a very enriching way. I want this book to give you the perspective and context that I have gained and benefited from, by listening to peoples wants and needs, their hopes and dreams as well as their frustrations in many different settings and relationships and then applying what I have learned through my disciplines; formal and informal; intellectual and creative; practical and spiritual. I have helped many people in understanding that much if not all of the answers, or the path to the answers to the questions or issues that trouble them already lie within them or are certainly within their capacity to realize and to grow from. I have helped them see what I have learned of the power of the individual spirit and how to tap into it and to understand the unique quality and beauty that lies within each of us. Guided by our philosophical underpinnings, seasoned by our experiences, and driven by our desire to grow and our aspirations for a brighter and more spiritually enriching future, we together share this glorious far flung flight through space on this water soaked life giving island of the cosmos we call home; children of the sun you and I; *As I See It.*

Thank you so very much. Peace,

Chris

AFTERWORD

As I See It is the culmination of my experiences as an executive in the world of business and as a stage and studio performer and writer. A blend of the analytic and the creative; the practical and the philosophical; it is the next step in a life that brought me to a point where I have both the resources and the opportunity to combine my diverse skills in a meaningful way for the enrichment and benefit of my readers and listeners.

As I See It is the natural and organic progression of my varied disciplines and interests that will act as my vehicle to continue to convey a meaningful and inspirational message of the value and power each person has to make this beautiful world a better place simply by being the best person that they can be and understanding keenly that the hero they most admire already lives within them. So very often, the frustration or anxiety people are feeling is really the yearning to find that part of *themselves* that completes how they envision their role in the world around them. By understanding that we are all more the same than we are different, as well as identifying ones own unique qualities and talents, the importance of that individual and the gifts that they can offer become apparent and the power of the individual is set free. It is through this inward journey that both the individual and our society as whole may benefit and grow.

BIBLIOGRAPHY

These are the few tangential references I make in the song lyrics and poetry of this book:

Songs:

Give Me Your Song – "Let fortune favor the foolish hearts…" – *Hamlet*; William Shakespeare.

Eagles Over Aberdeen – "Rachel warned of the "Silent Springs" to come…" – refers to *Silent Spring* by Rachel Carson – Houghton Mifflin 1962.

Poems:

Love One Another Even More – "glory is but grace…" – Johnathan Edwards – Philosophical theologian early to mid-1700's. Full quote is "Grace is but glory begun, and glory is but grace perfected."

Angels of Mercy – "Blessed are the peacemakers" – *The Holy Bible*; Jesus' Sermon on the Mount, Matthew 5:9. Full quote is "Blessed are the peacemakers, for they shall be called the children of God."

ABOUT THE AUTHOR

"Patience can only find her rest, when her quiet vigil has found its reward…"

While my formal training lies in the areas of business, finance and investing, my life has always lead me along the path of writing and expression. A path that taught me that obstacles can be overcome, spirits can be inspired and love can be shared with the power of the word, written or sung. My first best friend and confidant was my guitar. And while my relationship with that guitar brought me to perform for many, it wasn't until years after I taught myself to play, that I decided to sit down with pen, paper, and guitar to write about things as I saw them, or, as I felt them. And while some of my writings are in the poem or prose format, without the guitar, she is never, ever far away.

I am blessed to live in beautiful Southern California whose people, history and cultures are as diverse as her vast magnificent landscape.

I simply can't think of a more beautiful place to celebrate the gifts we are all given. No need to look for inspiration here, as she will find you.

I've found many answers, a few questions and yes even a few mysteries in this pursuit of writing about my journey, and wouldn't you know it, today, it's where I've found you!

Visit the *As I See It* web site:
www.cmentch.com

You can always find Chris' current and future music on iTunes, CD Baby and most online music services.

CPSIA information can be obtained at www.ICGtesting.com
Printed in the USA
LVOW06*0136170915

454404LV00002B/9/P